About the Author

Jennifer Tillock is a speech-language pathologist (SLP) with over 24 years of experience working with children in schools, and now works via teletherapy. Her passion lies in helping young people overcome communication challenges and reach their full potential.

Jennifer's dedication extends beyond the clinical setting. She is also the author of engaging children's communication books, designed to make therapy sessions fun and interactive.

When she's not empowering young minds, Jennifer enjoys her time as a writer under the pen name Christine Tellach, crafting captivating stories that blend genres like paranormal westerns and urban fantasy.

Jennifer embraces a life that balances tranquility and creativity. She resides in a rural setting, surrounded by nature, and finds inspiration from her spirited daughters, her devoted husband, and their zen farm dog.

As a lifelong learner and avid reader, Jennifer is constantly seeking new ways to improve her practice and inspire her readers.

Mrs. Speech's website: https://mrsspeechonline.blogspot.com

Christine Tellach's website: https://christinetellach.blogspot.com/

Facebook: https://www.facebook.com/profile.php?id=61556892726241

Instagram: https://www.instagram.com/mrs.speechonline/

Goodreads: https://www.goodreads.com/author/show/49549289.Jennifer_Tillock

Amazon Author:
https://www.amazon.com/stores/Jennifer-Tillock-MS-CCC-SLP/author/B0D2ZKR5KZ

Cover Art by:

Gerd Altmann (gear tree) Gerd Altmann/geralt/pixabay.com

Prawny (background) https://pixabay.com/users/prawny-162579/

Building Confident Communicators:
Talk It Out, Work It Out!

As a speech-language pathologist with over 24 years of experience, I've witnessed the impact of strong communication skills on children's lives. Unfortunately, many young people struggle to express themselves clearly and navigate social situations.

Talk It Out, Work It Out! was born from my passion for empowering children (ages 8+) to overcome these challenges. This engaging resource goes beyond simply presenting scenarios. It equips them with the tools they need to think critically, communicate effectively, and advocate for themselves in any situation.

Here's what makes this book unique:

- **Real-Life Scenarios:** Children tackle relatable situations, building confidence through practice. Each chapter begins with discussion prompts and practical tips to guide them towards effective communication and self-advocacy.
- **Essential Skills Development:** Learn to conquer conflicts, navigate safely, and build self-advocacy, and master communication skills – all in one resource!
- **Teaching guide: Each section (Younger and Older) includes ideas for guiding children through the scenarios and connecting to their own lives.**
- **Targeted Support:** Clear chapter structure revolves around common locations of safety and self-advocacy needs.
- **Supporting Resources:** Refer to the comprehensive rubrics and visual aids in the back of the book to further enhance discussion and measure progress.

Let's empower our children to become confident communicators! Talk It Out, Work It Out! offers a fun and interactive way to build essential social-emotional learning (SEL) skills that will benefit them at school, home, and beyond.

I'd love to hear your thoughts! Share your child's experience with #TalkItOutWorkItOut on social media.

Talk It Out, Work It Out! A Safety and Self-Advocacy Workbook for Ages 8+

Interactive Scenarios for School, Home, and the World

Jennifer Tillock, M.S. CCC-SLP

Mrs. Speech LLC

Print ISBN: 979-8-9906153-2-8

E-Book ISBN: 979-8-9906153-3-5

Any references to historical events, real people or real places are incidental.

First printing edition 2024

Jennifer Tillock

Mrs. Speech, LLC

christinetellach.blogspot.com

mrsspeechonline.blogspot.com

Table of Contents

Younger Scenarios: 2nd-5th Grade

Developing Social-Emotional Skills: Interactive Scenarios for Building Confidence (Grades 2-5)

This resource guide provides educators, SLPs, and parents with a collection of interactive scenarios designed to help children in grades 2-5 develop essential social-emotional learning (SEL) skills. These scenarios address common challenges children face in their daily lives, prompting critical thinking and discussion around topics like **communication, conflict resolution, internet safety, and self-advocacy.**

The Power of Interactive Scenarios:

- **Engaging and Accessible:** Scenarios provide a relatable and engaging context for children to explore social-emotional concepts.

- **Promoting Critical Thinking:** Discussing various possibilities within each scenario encourages children to think critically and consider potential consequences.

- **Developing Communication Skills:** The scenarios create opportunities for children to practice effective communication skills, including expressing needs, active listening, and assertiveness.

- **Building Problem-Solving Skills:** By brainstorming solutions and evaluating outcomes, children can develop their problem-solving skills in a safe and supportive environment.

Using the Scenarios Effectively:

These scenarios can be used in a variety of settings, including individual therapy sessions, classroom lessons, or family discussions. Here are some suggestions for implementation:

- **Read the scenario aloud** and encourage children to visualize the situation.

- **Ask guiding questions** from the provided sections to prompt discussion and critical thinking.

- **Role-play different solutions** to the scenario, allowing children to practice communication and social skills.

- **Discuss the consequences** of each potential solution to help children understand the impact of their choices.

- **Connect the scenarios to real-life experiences** to enhance understanding and application of learned skills.

- **Encourage finding multiple solutions** and comparing outcomes.

Exploring Safety Through Different Situations

This resource provides a variety of scenarios categorized by common situations children encounter, promoting social-emotional skill development through discussion and role-playing.

- **School:** Social exclusion, borrowing belongings, bullying, disagreements with classmates, expressing frustration during games, test anxiety, negative peer comments about work

- **Kitchen:** Accidental messes, asking for recipe help, using sharp utensils, sharing the kitchen with siblings, disagreements about meals, spilling food on family members, pressure to eat disliked foods, body image concerns related to cooking

- **Bathroom:** Sharing with siblings, needing help with personal hygiene, witnessing someone struggling, taking turns using the bathroom, disagreements about bathroom etiquette, asking someone to leave the bathroom politely, body image concerns, self-talk about appearance

- **Strangers:** Stranger danger, asking for directions, accepting gifts from strangers, older kids you don't know, being separated from parents, answering the door

- **Home:** Fire safety, choking hazards, power outages, cleaning products, family situations, weather safety

- **Around Town/Outside:** Getting lost, witnessing a crime, weather safety, fire safety, getting hurt, bicycle breakdown, pool safety, public bathrooms, being sick away from home, helmet safety, library, lost house key

- **Animals:** Caring for a pet, witnessing animal cruelty, fear of animals, dealing with aggressive animals, dog safety, wild animal safety, lost pet

- **Medical:** Doctor visits, vaccinations, nervousness about medical tests, being sick, being hurt, first aid, medicine safety, allergies, masks

- **Social:** Rejection, feeling left out, making new friends, bullying, unwelcome touching, social rules, peer pressure, settling differences, when to tell an adult

- **Internet/Social Media:** Cyber-bullying, online stranger danger, sharing personal information, clickbait, sharing copyrighted material, installing unknown software, screen time

In addition to the provided scenarios, consider creating your own scenarios based on common challenges faced by the children you work with.

By using these interactive scenarios and fostering open discussions, educators, SLPs, and parents can equip children with essential social-emotional skills that will benefit them throughout their lives.

Visuals

Visuals can be very useful for children in grades 2-5 when problem-solving scenarios. Here's why:

- **Concrete Representation:** Visuals provide a concrete representation of the scenario, making it easier for children to understand the situation and the characters involved. Pictures can help them visualize the setting, the characters' emotions, and the potential solutions.

Engagement and Focus: Visuals can make problem-solving activities more engaging and fun, especially for children who are more visual learners. They can capture attention and keep children focused on the task at hand. **Stimulating Creativity:** Images can spark creativity and help children come up with new ideas for solutions. Seeing different possibilities visually can encourage them to think outside the box and explore various approaches.

Here are some specific examples of how visuals can be used with problem-solving scenarios for this age group:

- **Simple Illustrations:** Use age-appropriate illustrations that depict the characters, setting, and key elements of the scenario.

- **Flowcharts:** Create flowcharts that visually represent the different steps involved in the scenario and the potential consequences of different choices.

- **Comic Strips:** Use comic strips to show the situation unfolding and different characters' reactions. This can be helpful for scenarios that involve communication and conflict resolution.

- **Emojis:** Emojis can be used to represent the characters' emotions in the scenario, helping children understand the social and emotional aspects of the situation.

It's important to choose visuals that are age-appropriate and directly related to the scenario. Here are some additional things to consider:

- **Complexity:** Keep visuals simple and easy to understand, avoiding too much clutter or detail.

- **Color:** Use bright and engaging colors to attract attention and make the visuals more appealing.

- **Relevance:** Ensure the visuals directly relate to the scenario and the problem-solving process.

By incorporating visuals effectively, you can enhance children's understanding, engagement, and creativity when working through social-emotional learning scenarios.

Jennifer Tillock M.S. CCC-SLP

School Safety Superstars – Tips for a Safe and Happy School Day!

School is a fun place to learn and play with friends, but it's important to be a safety superstar too! Here are some super easy tips to help you stay safe at school:

- **Be a Map Master:** Get to know your school layout! Learn where the exits, bathrooms, and your classrooms are. This will help you find your way around quickly and know where to go in case of an emergency.

- **Drill Like a Pro:** Pay attention during fire drills and lock-down drills. These drills help everyone practice what to do if something scary happens. Remember, drills are like practice games so we're all ready!

- **Hold Onto Your Hero Stuff:** Keep an eye on your backpack, lunchbox, and other things. Don't share them with strangers, and if something goes missing, tell your teacher or another grown-up right away.

- **See Something, Say Something:** If you see someone being mean to another kid, or something that doesn't seem right, tell a teacher, counselor, or another grown-up you trust. They can help keep everyone safe!

- **Crosswalk Champions:** When walking or biking to school, use the crosswalks like a champ! Look both ways before crossing the street and stay on the sidewalks whenever you can.

- **Kindness Crew:** Treat everyone at school with kindness, from your friends to your teachers. Remember, words and actions can hurt, so be respectful and play fair!

- **Online Safety Squad:** If your school uses computers or tablets, be a super safe surfer! Don't share your personal information online and don't talk to strangers in chatrooms.

- **Don't Be Shy, Tell a Grown-Up:** If you don't feel well or get hurt at school, let a teacher or another grown-up know! They can help you feel better and make sure you're okay.

- **Be Prepared, Be a Hero:** Pack a small first-aid kit with bandages and wipes in your backpack. You never know when you might be a hero and need to help a friend with a scrape!

- **Talk to Your Grown-Up Team:** Tell your mom, dad, or caregiver about your day at school. Let them know if anything worries you or if you have any questions about safety. They're your safety superheroes too!

By following these tips, you can be a school safety superstar and help keep yourself and your friends safe and happy all year long!

Scenarios

The fire alarm screeches loud like a fire truck siren! You're in the middle of a spelling test, trying to sound out the word "believe." Your pencil just snapped in two, and you only have one more word left.

Your class erupts in cheers as Ms. Johnson announces a bug building project! You stare at the colorful construction paper and pipe cleaners, but Ms. Johnson's instructions about wings and antennae sound like gibberish.

You're zooming through math problems on your caterpillar worksheet, feeling like a butterfly about to take flight. Then you hit a problem with a bunch of circles and squiggly lines. You scratch your head – what are you supposed to do with these?

Ms. Garcia asks, "Who can tell me about the different parts of a plant?" You raise your hand, but when she calls on you, her question sounds like a jumble of words. You know about flowers and leaves, but what was she asking exactly?

Ms. Hernandez gives a bunch of instructions about lining up and putting away markers, but you only remember the first part about putting your chair under your desk. Uh oh, what else did she say?

The teacher asks, "What is 5 + 7?" Everyone around you yells out answers, but you were busy drawing a cool robot in your notebook. Oops, what was the question?

The teacher asks everyone to copy some words from the board, but one word has loopy letters you've never seen before. It looks like a fancy noodle! What is that word?

You rush back to class after using the bathroom, but everyone is hunched over papers you don't have. Maybe they're secret treasure maps?

You're building a super cool volcano with red and orange paper mache, but you can't remember if you need to put the lava in first or the mountain.

There's a word on your science worksheet that looks like a tangled mess of letters – "photosynthesis." You sound it out in your head, but it comes out "funny toesynthesis." What is that word?

The class opens their books and starts reading. You look around – everyone seems to know what's going on, but you missed something! Did the teacher turn into a superhero and fly away while you were sharpening your pencil?

You skip out of the bathroom, ready to rejoin recess, but the classroom is empty! Where did everyone go? Did they all go to the playground without you? What is the problem?

The teacher asks everyone to check their work for mistakes with a red pen, but all you have is a blue one. Is your paper going to be all wrong because of the wrong pen color?

Mr. Jackson is talking about the rain forest, but his words are flying by your ears like a speeding cheetah! You try to listen, but everything sounds like a blur. What is the problem?

You raise your hand because you know the answer about explorers finding a new land. But when you open your mouth to speak, the word "continent" gets stuck on your tongue.

You come back from the bathroom to find the whole class looking grumpy and quiet. The teacher says they're in trouble for talking during a movie. But you weren't even there!

The scratchy voice on the speaker crackles to life. "Attention students, there will be a sign-up table in the cafeteria after lunch today for the spring talent show! Showcase your singing, dancing, or amazing magic tricks!" You glance around at your friends, but none of them seem to know what the talent show is.

You twist the dial on your locker, but the numbers just don't click into place. You try it again, starting from the beginning, but nothing! You hear your classmates slam their lockers shut and head off to class. You're starting to sweat a little.

The teacher drones on about the American Revolution, but the words seem muffled and far away. You squint at the board, but the letters blur together. Maybe you need glasses? Everyone else seems to be taking notes with ease.

Ms. Jones whispers instructions for the science experiment, but you only catch half of it. "Something, something, mix the baking soda with the vinegar…" You try to peek at your neighbor's paper, but they're focused on their own work.

Your stomach growls like a hungry bear. You forgot your lunch at home – again! You peek into your lunchbox, just in case there's a miracle granola bar hiding in the corner, but it's empty.

The teacher calls on you. Your mind races – wasn't the question about the different parts of a plant? You know the answer is on the tip of your tongue, but you need a second to remember the right word.

You reach for the tempting chocolate chip cookies, but the lunch lady plops a mystery scoop of something brown and mushy onto your tray. "Broccoli surprise!" she chirps. You don't even like regular broccoli, let alone surprise broccoli!

The line shuffles forward, but the person behind you keeps bumping into your backpack. It feels like they're practically pushing you! This isn't a mosh pit at a concert, it's the lunch line!

Ms. Garcia's brow furrows as she talks to you about your upcoming book report. Is it something you said? Did you forget to mention the main character's pet hamster? Her voice is getting a little higher pitched, and you can't tell if she's explaining something or mad at you.

Jennifer Tillock M.S. CCC-SLP

The white board is covered in writing, but it looks like gibberish. There are circles, squiggles, and weird symbols you've never seen before. Is this some kind of secret code? Everyone else seems to be copying things down, but you're totally lost.

Your heart beats faster as you reach the climbing wall. Everyone else looks so confident, but your palms are sweaty and your legs feel like jelly. What if you fall and everyone laughs?

The classroom door slams shut and the lights flicker. The teacher announces a "lock and teach" – the school is on lock-down! Everyone sits quietly at their desks, but you can't help but feel scared.

The bell rings for recess, and you race outside to join your friends. You dodge laughing kids and weaving jump ropes, but when you stop to catch your breath, you realize you're all alone. You don't see anyone you know. You remember the teacher mentioning a new playground area today, but you have no idea where it is.

Ms. Johnson smiles and asks everyone to take out their completed worksheets on fractions. Uh oh. You remember the colorful worksheet with the pictures of pizzas, but yours is blank at home on your desk. You were too busy building a LEGO castle last night!

The school bus rumbles to a stop and your friend waves goodbye from the window. You get in line, but when it's your turn to board, the bus driver says they're not your usual driver and doesn't recognize you. You explain you're supposed to be on this bus, but they aren't sure what to do.

It's a beautiful fall day, but then the loud screech of the fire alarm cuts through the classroom chatter. Everyone jumps up, grabbing their belongings, but you've never experienced a fire drill before. You don't know where to go or what to do.

There's a new student in your class named Benjamin. He sits by himself at lunch and doesn't join any games during recess. You remember how nervous you felt on your first day at a new school, and you want to be nice.

Your stomach churns and your head feels hot. You think you might throw up, but you're in the middle of art class, gluing sparkly buttons onto a construction paper monster. You're worried the teacher will get mad if you ask to leave.

It's crunch time on your math test, and you're almost finished with the last problem. Suddenly, with a loud snap, your pencil breaks in half! You look around but nobody has a spare, and the pencil sharpener is all the way across the room.

It's library day, and your heart sinks as you search your backpack for the book you borrowed two weeks ago. You can't find it anywhere! You remember promising the librarian you'd take good care of it.

Ms. Garcia announces it's show and tell day! Everyone brought in something special to share, but your mind goes blank. You can't remember what you were supposed to bring from home.

Butterflies flutter in your stomach – today's the day of class play tryouts! You really want the part of the brave knight, but you're afraid to mess up in front of everyone.

Kitchen

Kitchen Capers: Staying Safe While You Cook!

The kitchen is a fun place to whip up yummy treats, but safety always comes first! Here are some superhero tips to keep you safe while you're on your kitchen adventures:

- **Mighty Mitts:** Ovens and stoves get super hot! Always wear oven mitts or potholders when touching hot dishes or opening the oven door.

- **Sharp Side Down:** Knives are sharp superheroes, but they need to be treated with care. Keep them pointed down when you're not using them, and always cut on a sturdy cutting board, not your fingers!

- **Water Warriors:** If a pan catches fire, don't use water! Water can spread grease fires. Turn off the heat and smother the flames with a pot lid or baking soda. Remember, only grown-ups should handle fire extinguishers!

- **Tame the Flames:** Keep loose clothing, like scarves or shirts with long sleeves, away from the stovetop. You don't want them catching on fire by accident!

- **Cleanliness is Key!:** Clean up spills right away to avoid slipping and sliding. A messy kitchen can lead to falls!

- **Soap Power:** Wash your hands before you start cooking and after you touch raw food like meat or eggs. Germs can hide on your hands and make you sick!

- **Little Helpers, Big Rules:** Even the coolest mini chefs need grown-up supervision in the kitchen. Hot things and sharp tools are for grown-up hands only!

- **Cool Down Crew:** Let hot food cool down before you take a bite. You don't want to burn your mouth!

- **Electrical Experts:** Don't overload outlets or play with electrical cords. If something sparks or seems wrong, tell a grown-up right away!

- **Appliance Adventures:** Turn off appliances like mixers or blenders when you're done using them. Unplug them before you clean them too.

Remember, with a little care and these super tips, you can be a kitchen safety hero and have tons of fun cooking delicious food!

Jennifer Tillock M.S. CCC-SLP

Scenarios

Your lunch tray arrives, and you reach for the carton of milk. With a hopeful grin, you pop the straw in, ready for a refreshing drink. But as you take a sniff, your nose wrinkles – something sour tickles your senses. You take a cautious sip, and you spit it out. Definitely not a normal milk taste!

You're helping set the table for dinner, carefully balancing a glass of water in each hand. Suddenly, your foot catches on a corner of the rug, and with a crash, the glass clatters to the floor, shattering into a spiderweb of cracks. Water spills everywhere, soaking your socks and pooling around your feet.

Dinnertime! You reach into the cabinet for a can of your favorite childhood comfort food – Spaghetti-Os! Your stomach growls in anticipation, but the instructions say to heat it up first. Glancing around, you spot the microwave – perfect! But wait, is it okay to put metal in there?

Freshly baked cookies – the smell fills the kitchen with warmth and happiness. You reach into the oven to grab the baking sheet, but your hand searches in vain – the oven mitt is missing! The metal feels scorching hot through the thin fabric of your shirt.

The aroma of chocolate chip cookies fills the air as you plop globs of dough onto the baking sheet. Just as you're about to pop another one on, your hand slips, and the dough splatters onto the floor, landing with a soft plop right next to Fido's wagging tail.

You want to help frost cookies with your sibling, but you're worried they'll look messy again. Your sibling reminds you everyone loved the taste last time and suggests easier decorating ideas. How can you decorate the cookies to be fun and tasty, but also avoid a frosting explosion?

Milk and cookies – a classic duo! You pour yourself a glass of milk, dunk a delicious cookie, and head off to bed for the night. The next morning, you grab another carton for breakfast, only to find it warm and sour. Uh oh, you must have forgotten to put it away last night!

You're pouring yourself a bowl of cereal in the morning when the milk carton slips and spills all over the floor. There's a small puddle around the base of the cabinet, and you see an electrical outlet nearby.

You're making pancakes for breakfast, but the stove burner won't turn off no matter how much you twist the knob. Smoke starts to rise from the pan, and you feel a growing sense of panic.

The warm oven heat feels delightful on your back as you reach in to grab the cookie sheet. But as you pull it out, a searing pain shoots up your arm – you've brushed your hand against the hot metal. Your fingers turn bright red, and a stinging sensation sets in.

You smell the delicious aroma of freshly baked cookies coming from the oven. You can't wait to try them! But the cookies are still hot.

Dinner prep time! Following the recipe, you pop a box of macaroni and cheese in the microwave. You set the timer, press start, and wait for the delicious cheesy smell. But instead, a burning odor fills the air! You open the microwave to find sparks and flames dancing around the singed remains of your dinner.

You're helping make dinner and your mom hands you a knife to chop some vegetables. You're a little nervous – you don't want to cut yourself!

You're helping make dinner and reach for a utensil in the drawer. But as you grab it, the handle feels loose and wobbly.

You're following a science experiment recipe online that involves mixing baking soda and vinegar. It looks like fun, but you remember your teacher mentioning not mixing certain household chemicals.

You're reaching for a pot of boiling water on the stove to add some pasta. Suddenly, the handle feels loose and wobbly!

You're grabbing a snack from the pantry and find a bag of grapes. You love grapes, but you remember your teacher talking about choking hazards.

You're pouring yourself a glass of milk and chatting with your sibling. Suddenly, the milk spills all over the counter, running right next to the toaster that's plugged in!

You grab a Popsicle from the freezer, eager for a cool treat. The icy treat sticks to your fingers, sending a jolt of coldness that makes you yelp.

You're making breakfast for yourself, feeling proud of your independence. You pop the bread into the toaster and set the timer, but get distracted and forget about the toast. The timer dings, but the toast emerges black as charcoal, filling the kitchen with a smoky smell.

You're happily washing dishes, singing along to your favorite song, but get a little too enthusiastic with the sponge. Soapy water splashes everywhere, making the floor slippery and nearly toppling a plate off the counter!

You're having a pizza party with friends. Everyone's dipping their pizza slices into a bowl of marinara sauce. You see one friend double-dip their crust back into the bowl after taking a bite.

You're helping chop vegetables for dinner. You see your sibling using a dull knife that takes a lot of effort to cut through the carrots. You suggest sharpening the knife, but they want to hurry and just use more force

You're carefully chopping an apple for a fruit salad when the knife slips, sending a slice flying across the counter. Luckily, it misses you but lands splat on the wall with a sticky thud.

You're helping set the table for a family gathering, balancing a pitcher of juice and two

Jennifer Tillock M.S. CCC-SLP

glasses precariously in your hands. But halfway to the table, your grip falters. The juice jug tips over, drenching the tablecloth in a sticky red mess.

You're packing your lunch and decide to include some grapes for a healthy snack. But you forget to close the container tightly. By the time lunchtime arrives, your backpack is filled with loose grapes rolling around like tiny marbles.

You're helping decorate sugar cookies with your friend. You both dip a cookie in the red frosting and reach for the sprinkles container at the same time. Your hands bump, sending the sprinkles flying! Now there's a colorful mess all over the counter and floor.

You're helping make chili for dinner. Your job is to sprinkle the cheese on top. But you forget to wash your hands after handling the hot peppers. Now your fingers are burning!

You're making a delicious fruit salad with your mom. You grab a knife to cut a strawberry, but you're not sure how to hold it safely.

You're reheating leftover pizza for lunch. You put the leftover slice on a paper plate and shove it in the microwave. Just as you hit start, you remember seeing a spark when you put a metal fork in the microwave last week.

You're making a smoothie for breakfast. You add all the ingredients to the blender and turn it on high. But the lid wasn't on tight enough, and now there's a fruity mess all over the counter!

You're helping make a fruit salad, but some of the fruit feels hard and unripe. You know unripe fruit doesn't taste good, but you don't want to waste it.

You're helping to wash the dishes. You fill a pot with soapy water to clean, but get a little carried away. The water keeps rising, and before you know it, the pot overflows, creating a sudsy mess on the counter.

You're drying dishes with a dish towel. Suddenly, the towel catches on the sharp corner of a metal pot in the drying rack, ripping the towel.

You're following a recipe to make a delicious breakfast. You crack an egg into a bowl, but the shell breaks unevenly, sending a slimy piece of eggshell into the whites. You try to fish it out with your fingers, but accidentally poke the yolk, making a big mess!

You're making a delicious soup with your parent. The recipe calls for a specific herb, but you can't find it anywhere. You spot a small, leafy plant on the windowsill and wonder if it might be the right one.

You pack a delicious lunch for school, including a yogurt. But in the rush of getting ready, you forget to put the ice pack in your lunch bag and leave it on the counter. By the time you get get to lunch, the yogurt is warm.

You're making a yummy snack in the microwave when suddenly, the power goes out! The microwave shuts off, leaving you with a dark kitchen.

You open the refrigerator to grab a juice box, but a strange odor hits your nose. You check the shelves and find a container of forgotten leftovers with a slimy green film on top.

You're rummaging through the pantry for a snack and spot a can of beans in the back. The can looks a little rusty, and the expiration date is a year ago!

You're helping set the table for dinner and reach into the drawer for some knives. You see a knife sharpener sitting next to them, but you're curious about how it works.

You're baking cupcakes with your sibling. You can't wait to take them out of the oven and add frosting! But you reach for the oven mitt and realize it's damp from washing dishes earlier.

You're helping your parent carry a pot of hot soup to the table. Suddenly, you trip over a rug, and the pot wobbles! Hot soup spills everywhere, splattering your leg and the floor.

You're making ice cubes and reach into the freezer to grab the mold. But the metal is freezing cold! You hold on too long, and your finger starts to feel numb and tingly.

You're helping clean up after dinner. You reach into the cabinet for the dish soap, but accidentally grab the bottle of window cleaner! You squirt some onto a sponge before realizing your mistake.

You reach into the fridge for a can of soda, excited for the refreshing fizz. But you accidentally bump the can against the shelf, causing it to erupt in a foamy geyser! The soda sprays all over the kitchen, leaving a sticky mess behind.

Jennifer Tillock M.S. CCC-SLP

Bathroom

Bathroom Breakers: Keeping Safe in the Splash Zone!

The bathroom is where we get squeaky clean, but it can also get a little slippery! Here are some super-useful tips to keep you safe in the bathroom:

- **Tub Time Traction:** Be careful getting in and out of the tub, especially when it's wet. Use a bath mat for extra grip and ask for help if you need it.

- **Hot Stuff:** Water can get really hot, so always test the temperature with your hand before getting in the shower or bath. Remember, grown-ups should adjust the water heater to a safe temperature.

- **Lid on the Loot:** Keep the toilet lid closed when you're not using it. This keeps the bathroom fresh and prevents curious toys (or pets!) from taking a dip.

- **Medicine Cabinet Mystery:** Medicines look like candy, but they're not! Never take any medicine unless a grown-up gives it to you.

- **Sharp Objects Safeguard:** Razors, scissors, and other sharp things can be dangerous. Keep them out of reach in a drawer or cabinet where little hands can't grab them.

- **Electrical Safety Splash:** Don't use electrical appliances like hair dryers near water. Water and electricity don't mix!

- **Clean Champs:** Wash your hands with soap and water after using the bathroom to keep germs at bay.

- **Super Slippery Surfaces:** Clean up spills right away so no one slips and takes a tumble.

- **Shower Power:** Tell a grown-up if the shower gets too hot or the shower head seems broken.

- **Doorbell Duty:** If you're in the bathroom and someone rings the doorbell, don't open the door by yourself. Wait for a grown-up to come and check who it is first.

By following these bathroom breaker tips, you can be a bathroom safety superstar and keep bath time squeaky clean and safe!

Scenarios

You're soaking in the tub, enjoying a relaxing bubble bath. You hold your Kindle in one hand, completely absorbed in the exciting story on the screen. Suddenly, your fingers slip! With a splash, the Kindle tumbles out of your grasp and plunges into the bubbly water.

Bath time and tunes sound like a perfect way to unwind. You light some candles, fill the tub with warm water, and grab your favorite radio. But where to put it? The only flat surface seems to be the rim of the bathtub, balanced precariously close to the water.

Uh oh! Nature calls at school, and you rush into a stall. You finish up and press the flush handle – but nothing happens. You press it again, and again, but the toilet won't flush. To your horror, water starts to rise in the bowl and spill over onto the bathroom floor.

You're taking a relaxing bath with your favorite tunes playing on your phone. The music sounds great, but your phone is getting a little steamy from the hot water.

You're home alone, enjoying some peace and quiet. Suddenly, a terrifying gurgle fills the air. You rush to the bathroom to find the toilet overflowing! Water spews from the bowl, quickly spreading across the bathroom floor.

You're using the school restroom when your stomach starts to gurgle loudly. Uh oh! You have an upset stomach and need to use the stall, but the door doesn't lock properly.

Disaster strikes! You're texting your friend from the bathroom when your phone slips out of your hand. With a horrifying plop, it lands right in the toilet bowl!

You're taking a relaxing bath when you hear a dripping sound. You investigate and discover a leak coming from the faucet under the sink. Water is starting to pool on the bathroom floor.

You're drying your hair with your electric hairdryer. You reach down to unplug it from the socket, but the cord feels hot! Yikes!

You need some light to shave your legs in the morning. You reach up to turn on the bathroom light switch, but it feels wet! Zapping sounds like an unpleasant surprise.

You're shampooing your hair in the shower, lost in thought. Suddenly, a cold blast of water hits you! You realize your sibling has turned on the cold faucet without warning.

You reach for your hairdryer after a relaxing bath, ready to dry your hair. But as you lean over the tub to plug it in, your hand bumps the hairdryer, sending it tumbling into the water with a loud fizz!

Your nature's call hits at a friend's house, and you use their bathroom. You finish up and press the flush handle, but nothing happens! The toilet won't flush, and water starts to rise in the bowl.

Jennifer Tillock M.S. CCC-SLP

You're stepping out of the shower, feeling refreshed and ready to dry off. You reach for a fluffy towel on the rack, but as you take a step forward, your foot slips! The floor feels wet and soapy, sending a jolt of fear through you. You grab the sink for balance, hoping to avoid a fall.

You're helping your parents clean the overflowing medicine cabinet. There are so many bottles crammed together, their labels a confusing jumble of colors and tiny print. You worry about accidentally grabbing the wrong medication, especially since some bottles seem to have almost identical labels!

Excitement bubbles over as you prepare for a relaxing hot bath. You turn the faucet, eager to fill the tub with steaming water. But as the water starts flowing, you gasp – it feels scalding hot! You scramble to adjust the temperature, hoping to avoid a painful burn.

With a sigh of relief, you sink into the bathtub after a long day. You turn on the bathroom vent fan to clear the steam, expecting a refreshing blast of air. But instead, a strange burning smell fills the room.

You're brushing your teeth and hear your favorite song from your phone on the counter. The bathroom floor is wet.

You're at a friend's house, and you use their bathroom. The toilet handle feels loose and wobbly.

You're taking a bath and notice the water level gets close to spilling over as you sit down.

You're brushing your hair and accidentally knock over a bottle of shampoo. The slippery shampoo spills all over the floor! How can you make the floor safe again?

You're trying to style your hair for a special occasion. You grab your mom's hairspray and give it a quick spritz. But you forget to point the nozzle away from your face, and a cloud of hairspray blasts you in the eyes! Ouch!

You're playing pretend bath time with your bath toys. You accidentally knock over a bottle of bubble bath solution, creating a colorful puddle on the floor.

You're sharing a bath with your sibling. They adjust the faucet without telling you, and suddenly the water feels very hot!

You're putting your toothbrush away after brushing your teeth. But you're in a hurry and accidentally knock it off the sink. It lands with a plop in the toilet bowl!

You grab a bar of soap from the dish in the shower, ready to lather up. But the soap is wet and slippery! It pops out of your hand and lands on the floor with a splat.

You're getting ready for bed and need to take your allergy medicine. But your medicine cabinet is cluttered, and several bottles look similar.

You're cleaning the bathroom sink after brushing your teeth. You reach for the sponge, but it feels slimy and smells a little funky!

You're looking for a new bath toy in the bathroom cabinet. You climb on a stool to reach a high shelf, but the stool wobbles precariously. Before you know it, you're losing your balance and about to fall!

You're taking a bath and hear someone trying to open the bathroom door. You don't recognize the voice.

You're getting ready for school and need to see the mirror to brush your hair. But the bathroom is full of steam and the mirror is completely fogged up!

You're helping your mom clean the bathroom. There are so many colorful bottles on the counter, and some look alike! You accidentally pick up the wrong bottle and almost squirt the liquid in your eye.

The bathroom light bulb burns out, leaving the room dark and spooky. You reach for a new bulb on the shelf, but it's way too high for you to grab safely.

You get out of the shower and reach for the towel, but as you bring it close to dry off your face you notice it smells bad.

You're drying your hair after a bath, feeling proud of your independence. But as you plug in the hairdryer, it sparks and makes a scary buzzing noise!

You're getting older and want to start shaving your legs like your older sibling. You find their razor in the bathroom cabinet. But razors are sharp!

Jennifer Tillock M.S. CCC-SLP

Stranger

Stranger Danger Detectives: Keeping Safe Around Unfamiliar People!

The world is full of amazing people, but sometimes you might meet someone you don't know well. Here are some super-secret detective skills to help you stay safe:

- **The "No - Go - Tell" Code:** This is your secret weapon! If someone you don't know well makes you feel uncomfortable, say NO in a firm voice. Go away from them and find a grown-up you trust, like a teacher, parent, or store employee. Then tell them what happened.

- **The "Buddy System":** There's power in numbers! Whenever possible, play with a friend or sibling, especially outside. It's more fun and safer to explore together.

- **The "Off-Limits" List:** Talk to your grown-ups about places you shouldn't go alone. This might include parks after dark, empty hallways, or anywhere you can't be easily seen.

- **The "Gift Refusal Reflex":** Strangers shouldn't give you gifts or candy. It's okay to politely say "no thank you" and tell a grown-up about it.

- **The "Personal Info Protection Shield":** Your personal information is like a secret code! Don't share your name, address, or phone number with people you don't know well.

- **The "Never Go Anywhere" Rule:** Never go anywhere with someone you don't know well, even if they offer you a ride, a puppy, or seem super nice. Remember, grown-ups will always ask your parents' permission first.

- **The "Trust Your Gut Feeling":** If you feel scared or uncomfortable about someone, even a little bit, listen to your instincts! It's okay to walk away and find a grown-up.

Not Sure if Someone is a Stranger?

Sometimes you might meet someone new, but you're not sure if they're a stranger or not. That's okay! This is where your grown-up detective skills come in. If you're not sure, ask your mom, dad, or another grown-up you trust if it's okay to talk to this person.

By using these stranger danger detective skills, you can stay safe and have exciting adventures with the people you know and trust! Remember, your grown-ups are always there for you, so don't hesitate to tell them if anything makes you feel uncomfortable.

Scenarios

You're walking home from school, humming a tune, when a car pulls up beside you. The driver leans out the window with a friendly smile. "Hi there! Your mom asked me to pick you up today."

You're playing a fun online game and meet someone who seems really nice. They tell you they live close by and want to meet up in person. What should you do if someone you met online asks to meet in real life?

You're drying your hands in the public bathroom at the museum after a fun afternoon. You finish drying and step aside to let the person behind you use the hand dryer. But when you move, a group of older kids rushes in and cuts you in line, hogging the hand dryers and laughing loudly.

You're walking home from school when you see a stranger sitting on a park bench, looking lost and sad. They tell you they're waiting for their mom, but she's taking a long time.

You're playing outside when your neighbor, Mr. Thompson, offers to take you to the park for ice cream. Your mom told you not to go anywhere with him without her permission, but Mr. Thompson seems really nice.

You're at school playing with a group of kids. They all have cool new trading cards, and they keep pressuring you to show them yours. You don't feel comfortable sharing them, but you don't want to seem like a spoilsport.

An adult you don't know very well offers you a candy bar. Your parents taught you not to take treats from strangers.

Your friend whispers a secret in your ear on the playground. They tell you they'll get you in big trouble if you tell anyone. Secrets can be exciting, but they can also be uncomfortable. What should you do if someone tells you a secret that makes you feel uncomfortable?

You're walking home from school when you see a shiny new toy car on the sidewalk. There's no one around, and it looks amazing! But you know it's not a good idea to take things that don't belong to you.

You're happily singing along to your favorite music on your phone while using a stall in a public bathroom at the mall. Suddenly, you hear a woman's voice from the next stall. "That's my ringtone too! Great taste in music!" You're a little surprised, but you politely say hi back. The conversation continues, and the woman starts asking you personal questions.

You're at the park, happily playing on the swings. An older kid you don't know walks over and tells you that you're playing wrong. They try to show you a "new way" to swing, but it looks dangerous. What should you do if someone tries to pressure you into playing in a way that feels unsafe?

You're at the library with your friend when they spot a restricted section with books that look interesting. They suggest you sneak a peek even though there's a sign that says "Adults Only."

It's a fun day at the fair with your family. You wander off to explore a bit and get separated from your parents in the bustling crowd. You start to feel lost and a little scared.

Your neighbor, Mr. Thompson, waves from across the street. "Hey there! How about a cookie to help with those after-school blues?" he calls out, holding up a plate of warm, chocolate chip cookies.

You're using a public bathroom at the park when you hear a muffled thump outside the stall. You peek out cautiously and see a small, wrapped package left on the floor next to the sinks. There's no one else in the bathroom, and you have no idea who left it.

You're walking home, kicking a pebble back and forth, when you realize you're being followed. You glance back and see someone a few houses behind you, walking at the same pace.

Someone knocks on the door. You cautiously peer through the window and see a person you don't recognize standing on the porch. They knock again, a little louder this time.

At the park, you're swinging back and forth when an older kid you don't know walks over. He offers you candy and asks you to come play behind the bushes.

You're in a single-occupancy bathroom at the movie theater. You've just locked the stall door when you hear the handle jiggle and the lock rattle. A stranger's voice calls out, "Is anyone in there?" You feel a knot of worry in your stomach.

You're at the mall with your mom, looking at toys, when you realize you can't find her anywhere.

The phone rings while you're home alone. You pick it up, and a stranger asks for your mom. They say they have a surprise for her.

You're enjoying a refreshing dip in the pool at the community center. You take a break to grab a towel, but when you turn around, you can't see your parent anywhere.

You're on the swings at the park, having a blast. An older kid you don't know pushes you extra hard, making you feel scared and unsafe.

You're using a public bathroom at the pool. As you're leaving the stall, a group of much older teenagers are gathered by the only exit, blocking the way. They seem loud and rowdy, and you feel a little scared.

You're waiting for the school bus after school, feeling a little nervous because you're alone. A stranger sits down next to you and starts asking you questions about your day.

It's Halloween night! You're trick-or-treating with your friends when you come to a house with a bowl of candy outside, but no adult around.

Jennifer Tillock M.S. CCC-SLP

You're waiting for the bus after school when a car pulls up and a stranger asks if you need a ride.

You're walking home from school with a heavy backpack when a stranger offers to help you carry it. They seem friendly, but something feels off.

You're at the park, happily playing on the swings. An unfamiliar adult approaches you, offering to push you higher. You don't know this person, and they seem a little too eager to help.

You're walking home from school when you see a teenager sitting alone on a park bench, crying. They claim they're lost and their phone is dead. They ask you to use your phone to call their mom for them.

You're playing outside your house when an older kid you don't know walks by. They start bragging about a cool new video game and invite you to come inside their house to see it. You're curious, but your parents told you not to go into strangers' homes.

You're washing your hands at the airport bathroom before your flight. A woman approaches you, looking flustered. "Excuse me," she says, "Have you seen my little brother? He's about your age and wearing a blue jacket." You haven't seen anyone, but she seems genuinely worried.

You're walking home from school when you see someone familiar approaching from behind. It's the person you met at the park the other day who offered you candy. They seem friendly, but you remember your parent's warnings about strangers.

You're home alone when the doorbell rings. You look through the peephole and see a delivery person holding a package. You're expecting a package, but your parents told you not to open the door for strangers.

You're playing soccer at the park, focused on the game. Suddenly, a car horn beeps, and a stranger waves from the window. They offer you a ride home, even though it's close by. What should you do if someone offers you a ride you don't need?

You're walking your dog in the park when someone approaches with a sad look. They claim they lost their pet, which looks suspiciously similar to yours. They ask to touch your dog for a closer look.

It's Halloween night! You're trick-or-treating with friends when you see a decorated house with a bowl of candy far from the porch. No adult is around.

You're waiting for soccer practice, sitting alone. A stranger asks if you've seen their phone and offers a reward if you can help find it.

You're enjoying the monkey bars at the park when older kids approach, teasing and making you feel uncomfortable.

You're walking your dog in the park when someone approaches you, crying and saying they lost their pet. They ask if you've seen a dog that looks exactly like yours.

Home

Home Alone Heroes: Keeping Safe When You're on Your Own!

Even though your home is your cozy castle, there are still some safety things to remember when you're playing by yourself. Here are some tips to turn you into a home alone hero:

- **Master of the Mighty Mitts:** Do you know where the oven mitts are? Even though it's not the kitchen, remember hot things can be anywhere, like a lightbulb or a heat lamp. Be careful and ask a grown-up for help if you need to touch something hot.

- **Climbing Champions:** Climbing furniture is super fun, but it can also be a recipe for tumbles! Play on the floor or in designated climbing areas like jungle gyms.

- **Sharp Object Shields:** Scissors, knives, and other sharp things can be dangerous if not handled properly. Leave them alone and let a grown-up use them for you.

- **Electrical Experts:** Outlets and cords are not for playing! Don't stick anything in them and keep electrical cords away from water. If something sparks or seems wrong, tell a grown-up right away!

- **Window Wanderers:** Open windows are cool, but they can also be dangerous. Don't climb on windowsills or lean out too far.

- **Welcome Wagon Worries:** The doorbell might ring, but don't open the door by yourself! Grown-ups will answer the door. If you want to know who it is, ask a grown-up to use the peephole or talk through the door.

- **Medicine Mix-Up Mayhem:** Medicine bottles might look like juice boxes, but they're not! Never take any medicine unless a grown-up gives it to you.

- **Choking Champions:** Be careful with small toys, balloons, and other things that could fit in your nose or mouth. These can be choking hazards!

- **Firefighter Friends:** Smoke detectors are your fire fighter friends! If the smoke alarm goes off, don't hide under the covers. Meet your grown-up in your family's meeting place outside (practice this with your grown-ups beforehand!).

- **Power Play:** Electronics are fun, but too much screen time can be bad for your eyes. Follow your grown-up's rules about how much screen time you get each day.

By following these home alone hero tips, you can be safe and have tons of fun while you're playing by yourself! Remember, if you ever feel unsure about something, don't hesitate to call a grown-up for help.

Scenarios

Dinnertime arrives, and your stomach growls. You look at your big brother hopefully. "Pasta night, please!" you plead. But your brother wrinkles his nose. "Nope, I'm in the mood for Chinese takeout!"

You're playing a board game with your family when you hear a strange crackling sound coming from the kitchen. You peek in and see smoke billowing from the toaster. The smoke alarm starts blaring!

Disaster strikes! You're getting ready for school when you zip up your pants – but the zipper gets stuck halfway. You wiggle and jiggle, but it won't budge.

The front door closes with a click as your parents leave for their evening errands. You're home alone for the first time!

You're home alone when the doorbell rings. You peek through the peephole and see a stranger standing there holding a package. You weren't expecting anything, and your parents told you not to open the door to strangers.

A sharp scent stings your nostrils as you walk through the house. Smoke! You look around frantically, searching for the source.

Suddenly, the entire house plunges into darkness. The power is out! You stand frozen for a moment, then scramble to find something to light your way.

You walk in the front door and wrinkle your nose. A strange, unpleasant odor hangs in the air. It smells like rotten eggs, but you haven't cooked any in weeks.

The fire alarm goes off when you are asleep. You check your bedroom door and it is hot and smoke is coming through the cracks. You are on the second story of your house.

You're watching a movie with your family when a loud, high-pitched whine suddenly fills the air. Your parents turn on the TV news, and there's a tornado warning for your area! The screen shows a dark, swirling funnel cloud approaching your town.

You're curled up on the couch, reading a book, when a knock on the door startles you. You jump up and walk cautiously to the door. Who could it be?

You're helping your parent clean the kitchen. You're assigned to wipe down the table, but the spray bottle you're using makes the whole room smell like lemons. It makes your eyes water and your nose itch.

You're getting ready for bed and decide to light a scented candle to make your room smell nice. But then you get called downstairs for dinner and forget about the candle burning.

You're relaxing on the couch when you notice a strange, chemical smell coming from the kitchen. You investigate and find a container spilled on the floor, leaking a weird-colored liquid.

It's chore time! You forgot to take out the trash yesterday, and now the bag is overflowing.

You're home alone watching TV when you hear glass breaking from another room. It sounds like it might have been a window.

Your grumpy uncle arrives for a visit. He gives you a big, tight hug even though you don't feel like it. You feel a little uncomfortable, but you don't want to hurt his feelings. What should you do if someone gives you a hug when you don't want one?

The fire alarm goes off when you are asleep. You check your bedroom door and it is hot, and smoke is coming through the cracks. You are on the 3rd floor of an apartment.

You're hungry for popcorn, so you grab a bag and put it in the microwave. But you accidentally set the timer for the wrong setting!

You're making a delicious snack in the kitchen when you hear a knock at the door. You peek through the peephole and see a stranger holding a clipboard. They say they're here to check the smoke detectors, but you weren't expecting anyone.

You're playing outside in the backyard when you accidentally lock yourself out of the house. You don't have a key, and your parents won't be back for hours.

It's family game night, but your little brother keeps losing and starts getting grumpy.

You're playing a game on your tablet when the phone rings. It's an unknown number, but you answer it because you're curious. The person on the other end sounds friendly and asks for your name.

You're playing on the floor with your toys when your pet steps right in the middle of your creation!

You can't find your favorite stuffed animal anywhere! You've looked everywhere you can think of.

The fire alarm goes off when you are asleep. You check your bedroom door and it is hot and smoke is coming through the cracks. You are on the first story of your house.

It's cleaning day, and you're assigned to wipe down the kitchen counters. You see a spray bottle with a skull and crossbones symbol – it looks scary!

You're playing in your room when a loud beeping sound fills the air. The smoke alarm is going off!

You are home alone when you hear the tornado siren go off outside your house.

You're home alone and in the middle of an exciting video game when the lights suddenly flicker and then go out completely. Everything is plunged into darkness! You hear the faint hum of the refrigerator stop, and you realize the power is out. The house is dark, and you can't see anything.

Jennifer Tillock M.S. CCC-SLP

The fire alarm goes off when you are asleep.
You check your bedroom door and it is not hot,
but smoke is coming through the cracks. You
are on the second story of your house.

You're not feeling well – your tummy hurts,
and you have a fever. You want to play video
games, but you know you should rest.

You and your family are planning what to do
for the weekend. Everyone wants to do
something different, and you can't agree.

Around Town/Outdoor

Sidewalk Superstars: Staying Safe on Your Outdoor Adventures!

The world outside is full of exciting things to explore, but there are also some safety tips to remember so you can be a sidewalk superstar! Here are some super-useful skills to keep you safe on your outdoor adventures:

- **Sun Shield:** The sun can be our friend, but it can also give us sunburn. Wear sunscreen whenever you're outside, especially on sunny days.
  - **Bonus Tip:** Ask a grown-up to help you reapply sunscreen throughout the day!
- **Hydration Heroes:** Just like plants need water, so do you! Carry a water bottle with you and take sips often, especially on hot days. Feeling thirsty is a sign you need more water!
- **Sidewalk Savvy:** Sidewalks are for walking, not biking or scooting! These are safer for designated areas like parks or bike paths.
- **Traffic Tamers:** Look both ways before crossing the street, even at crosswalks. Wait for the walk signal and cross with a grown-up whenever possible.
- **Playground Power:** Playgrounds are for fun, but they can also have bumps and falls. Be careful on equipment and follow the playground rules.
- **Wheeled Wonder Safety:** Whether you're riding a bike, scooter, or skateboard, wear a helmet that fits snugly! It can protect your head in case of a fall.
- **Hot Pavement Heroes:** Asphalt gets really hot on sunny days! It can burn your feet, so wear shoes whenever you're outside.
- **Weather Warriors:** Be prepared for changing weather! If it starts to rain or storm, head inside or find shelter. Don't play outside during lightning or strong winds.
- **Nature Detectives:** The great outdoors is full of cool things to see, but be careful not to touch plants or animals you don't know. Some might irritate your skin or even be poisonous.

Lost and Found Foxes:

If you ever get lost outside, like at a park or playground, don't panic! Here's what to do:

- **Try to Find Your Grown-Up:** First, look around for your grown-up. If you can see them, call out to them and walk towards them slowly.

- **Find a Trusted Grown-Up:** If you can't find your grown-up, try to find another grown-up you trust, like a store employee, park ranger, or security guard. Someone who looks like they are working at a store or official building is a good choice.

- **Look for a Mom with Kids:** If you can't find any grown-ups you already know, look for a mom with kids. Moms with kids are usually good choices for help because they are likely looking out for their own children too.

- **Stay Put:** If you can't find anyone to help, stay put in a safe spot. Don't wander around looking for your grown-up.

- **Get Attention:** If you see someone safe, try to get their attention by waving your arms or calling out for help.

- **Remember Your Information:** It's a good idea to memorize your home phone number or address in case you get lost and lose your phone.

By following these sidewalk superstar tips, you can explore the world outside safely and have tons of fun on your outdoor adventures! Remember, your grown-ups are always there to help you stay safe, so don't hesitate to ask them if you have any questions.

Scenarios:

You're at the store with your mom who's buying groceries. She leaves you in line while she runs back for something. You don't have any money, and it's almost your turn to pay.

You're playing on the monkey bars at recess when you see a younger kid struggling to climb down. They seem scared and unsure what to do.

You're happily playing on the slide when a bigger kid shoves you out of line. You land in the sand and feel hurt and angry.

You're hiking with your friends on a new trail, but the path seems to be getting narrower and steeper than you expected. You're starting to feel uncomfortable and unsure if you can continue.

You're at the library excited to pick out some new books, but you realize you've forgotten your library card at home.

You're engrossed in the movie, popcorn halfway to your mouth, when a jarring alarm shatters the silence. Red flashing lights paint the screen, and a disembodied voice announces "Evacuate the building!" Confusion ripples through the crowd – is it real, or part of the movie? Uncertainty lingers as you glance at your friends, unsure of what to do next.

You are outside playing when you fall and hit your mouth. You can feel your tooth is wiggly.

You're on a nature walk with your class when you accidentally step on a bee! It stings your ankle, and it starts to swell up and hurt.

You're lost in a maze of bookshelves at a giant bookstore. You can't find the exit or your parents anywhere, and your phone battery is dead.

You're playing basketball at the park with friends when you see an emergency alert on your phone about a flash flood warning. The skies look clear, but you know flash floods can happen quickly.

You're waiting in line for pizza with your friend at the food court, but when you reach the front, you realize you forgot your wallet at home. Your friend doesn't have enough money to cover both meals.

You're at a Fourth of July celebration with your family, enjoying the fireworks display. Suddenly, a loud boom sends a spark flying, landing right on your shoe.

You're enjoying a bike ride with your friends when you hear a hiss and realize you have a flat tire. You don't have a spare tube or pump, and you're miles from home.

You're happily playing on the swings when a younger child tries to climb onto the swing while it's still moving. You explain it's dangerous, but they keep trying to push their way on.

You're at the store looking for something on a shelf, but an elderly woman is blocking the way with her cart. She's carefully examining all the labels.

You're separated from your parents at the fair, but you remember they mentioned they were going to watch the pig races next. The fair is loud and crowded, and you don't know where the pig races are located.

You're using a public restroom at the park before a soccer game. Everything is going well, but as you wash your hands, you hear the dreaded "click" of an empty toilet paper dispenser. Uh oh! You know there might not be anyone else in the bathroom, and the game starts soon.

The blaring fire alarm shatters the calm browsing. Smoke curls from behind a clothing rack, and you see flickering orange flames licking at the display. Panic bubbles in your chest – you need to get out, now!

You're browsing the shelves in a bookstore when you hear a loud crash and see fallen books blocking the exit. People are starting to panic. What should you do if you're in a bookstore when there's a minor earthquake or another unexpected event that causes a blockage?

You're splashing around in the pool with your friends when you notice a younger child struggling to stay afloat and looking scared. There's no lifeguard on duty.

It's a fun day at the fair with your family. You wander off to explore a bit and get separated from your parents in the crowd. You start to feel lost and a little scared.

You're at the movie theater with a friend. You're both hungry, but you forgot to bring any extra money. During the previews, you see a group of older kids leaving the theater and leaving behind a half-eaten bag of popcorn on their seat. You're tempted to grab it.

You're on a thrilling rollercoaster ride with your friend, but halfway through, you feel sick to your stomach. You're worried you might throw up.

You're walking quickly through the mall, excited to meet your friend, when you trip over a loose shoelace and fall. Your knee scrapes on the ground, and tears well up in your eyes.

You're thirsty after playing soccer practice and head to the water fountain. You press the button, but only brown water sputters out.

You are at the movies with a friend. You excitedly grab your ticket to see the new animated movie, but when you enter the theater, you realize it's actually a scary movie playing.

You're outside having a blast playing tag. You're chasing your friend around the tree when suddenly the bright sunshine disappears for a moment. You look up and see a flash of lightning zigzag across the sky! It's loud and a little scary.

You're on a bike ride with a friend when their bike chain snaps, leaving them stranded.

Jennifer Tillock M.S. CCC-SLP

You're miles away from home and don't have any tools.

You're at a friend's house for a party when you notice there are no clear emergency exits visible. The house seems like a maze of rooms and hallways.

You're riding your bike on the path when you see a group of older kids blocking the way. They're swerving back and forth and don't seem to be paying attention to other riders.

You finally reach the front of the line at the fast-food restaurant, ready to order your favorite burger. But when you try to use the touch-screen menu, none of the buttons seem to work.

You're at the bowling alley and really need to use the restroom. The single-stall bathroom has a keypad entry system, but you don't see a code posted anywhere.

You're on a hike with your family, enjoying the scenery. You stop to take a picture, but when you look up, you don't recognize the trail anymore.

You're on a school trip to a museum, exploring the exciting exhibits with your class. You get distracted by a cool display and accidentally wander away from the group. The museum seems big and confusing now.

You're riding your bike on the path when you see a group of kids skateboarding recklessly ahead. They're weaving in and out of traffic and don't seem to be paying attention.

You're waiting in line for pizza with your friend at the food court, but when you reach the front, they realize they forgot their wallet at home.

You search everywhere for your favorite stuffed animal you brought to the library, but it's vanished. You check the lost and found, but it's empty. You remember you have a picture of yourself with the stuffed animal on your phone.

You need to use the library computer to finish your school project, but all the computers are occupied. You see someone leave a computer, but they haven't logged out yet.

You're using a public restroom when your stomach starts to gurgle and you realize you urgently need to use the stall. But all the stalls are occupied, and there's a line forming outside the door.

You're playing basketball in the driveway and accidentally shoot the ball too high. It crashes through a neighbor's window! You feel scared and unsure of what to do.

You're at a thrilling amusement park with your family. You wait in line for a rollercoaster ride, but when you get off, you can't find your parents anywhere in the crowd.

You're enjoying a movie with your family when you hear a loud CRACK! You look down and see you've stepped on someone's popcorn bucket, spilling buttery kernels everywhere.

You're at the park with your friends and see a cool new skateboard they brought. You really want to try it, but you don't have your helmet with you.

You're walking home from school and find a phone lying on the sidewalk. You're curious to see who it belongs to, but it's password-protected.

You're enjoying a refreshing dip in the pool at the community center. You take a break to grab a towel, but when you turn around, you can't see your parent anywhere.

You're using a public bathroom stall at the library after finishing a great book. Suddenly, the stall door clicks shut and locks! You try the handle, but it's jammed. You're alone in the bathroom, and a wave of panic washes over you.

You're happily browsing books at the library when you realize you've wandered into a quiet section you don't recognize. You feel a little lost and unsure of which way to go.

You're at the library searching for books for a school report. The computer says a specific book should be on a certain shelf, but it's nowhere to be found.

You're at a restaurant with an empty lemonade glass. You'd love another one, but your server hasn't been around in a while.

You're swinging high on the swings when your shoe flies off and lands precariously on the top of the climbing frame. You can't reach it, and you don't want to climb down without your shoe.

You're at a fast-food restaurant craving a burger. The problem? You hate the sauce they always put on it.

You ordered something new at a restaurant, but when you take a bite, it tastes off – like the meat might be spoiled.

You're walking home from school, but you realize you've lost your house key somewhere along the way. Your parents won't be home for a couple of hours.

You're at the mall with your mom, trying on clothes. You pick out a shirt you love, but you can't find your mom anywhere. You start to feel a little nervous.

You're playing soccer with friends, and the ball rolls into the street.

You get off the bus stop, but realize you might have gotten off at the wrong place. The bus has already left.

You want to ride your bike to the convenience store down the street. What are some safety tips to remember?

Jennifer Tillock M.S. CCC-SLP

Animals

Wild Wonders: Keeping Safe Around Wild Animals!

The world is full of fascinating animals, and that includes our furry (or feathery, or scaly!) friends at home – pets! Here are some super-important tips to keep you safe and keep the animals happy on your outdoor adventures:

- **Leave Wild Animals Wild:** Admire animals from a safe distance! Don't approach, touch, or try to feed them. They might seem cute and cuddly, but they can scratch, bite, or even carry diseases.

- **Respect Their Space:** If an animal seems scared or agitated, back away slowly and give them plenty of space. Never corner or chase an animal.

- **Be Aware of Your Surroundings:** Before you head out on a hike or explore a new area, ask a grown-up if there are any wild animals to be aware of.

- **No Food for Friends:** Never feed wild animals, even if they look hungry. Human food can make them sick, and they might start to associate people with food, leading to dangerous situations.

- **Supervise Your Squad:** If you're outside with pets, keep them on a leash and under your control. This protects them from wild animals and stops them from bothering wildlife.

- **Know Before You Go:** If you're visiting a zoo or animal park, follow all the rules and stay behind barriers. Don't tap on the glass or try to get the animals' attention.

- **Home Alone Heroes:** If you see a wild animal near your house, don't go outside to investigate. Tell a grown-up right away!

- **Be Alert:** While you're exploring outdoors, be aware of your surroundings. Listen for animal sounds and watch out for signs of wildlife, like tracks or droppings.

- **Watery Wisdom:** If you're near water, be careful! Don't swim in areas where there might be alligators, crocodiles, or other water dangers.

Pet Pals: Keeping Safe with Our Furry Friends

Pets are our companions, but it's important to remember they are animals with instincts too. Here are some tips to keep you and your pet safe and happy:

- **Gentle Giants:** Be gentle with pets, especially if they're new to you or seem scared. Avoid grabbing, pulling, or poking them. Let them sniff your hand first and get comfortable with you.

- **Playful Pals:** Playtime with pets should be fun and positive! Use pet-safe toys and avoid roughhousing or teasing, which can lead to nipping or scratching.

- **Respect Their Space:** Even pets need some alone time. If your pet growls, hisses, or tries to hide, give them space and let a grown-up know.

- **Supervise Snack Time:** Don't share your food with pets unless a grown-up says it's okay. Some human foods can be dangerous for them.

- **Leash Law Legends:** Always use a leash when walking your pet outside, especially in unfamiliar areas. This keeps them safe from traffic and other animals.

- **Clean Up Crew:** Clean up after your pet! This helps keep them healthy and prevents the spread of diseases.

- **Talk to the Owner:** If you see someone with a pet you want to touch, be sure to talk to the owner about whether the animal is safe to touch, and how to touch it. Remember, just because your pets are friendly doesn't mean everyone's pets are safe to touch.

Encountering an Unfamiliar Dog:

If you see an unfamiliar dog approaching you, here's what to do:

- **Stay Calm:** Don't run! Running can trigger a chase instinct in some dogs.

- **Stand Tall:** Stand still and tall, like a tree. Avoid making eye contact or bending down.

- **Be Quiet:** Don't yell or scream. This can scare the dog further.

- **If Knocked Over:** If the dog knocks you down, curl up into a ball and protect your head with your hands. Stay still until the dog loses interest and leaves.

Remember: Most dogs are friendly, but it's important to know how to react if you encounter an unfamiliar one. By following these tips, you can help keep yourself safe.

Always tell a grown-up if a dog barks at you, chases you, or tries to bite you.

Jennifer Tillock M.S. CCC-SLP

Scenarios

You're at the park and see someone walking a really cute dog. You'd love to pet it, but you don't know the dog.

You're playing outside your house when a neighbor's dog runs into your yard. You don't know the dog well, and it seems a little scared.

You're at the park having a blast on the swings. You push yourself high and giggle as you fly through the air. Suddenly, you hear a barking sound getting closer and closer. A big, brown dog you don't know comes running towards you, barking excitedly.

You go to the back door to go play in the backyard, when you notice a fox under one of the bushes.

You're playing soccer in the backyard with friends, and the ball ends up in your neighbor's yard. You know they sometimes have a dog in there.

You're at the dentist's office and see a calming fish tank in the waiting room. You tap on the glass to get the fish's attention, but another kid reminds you that tapping the tank can stress the fish.

You're relaxing on the beach with your friends, building sandcastles. Suddenly, a seagull swoops down and tries to snatch your sandwich!

You just read a story in class about a boy and his beloved dog. The story ended sadly, with the dog passing away. Now you're worried about your own pet.

You're hiking with your family when you spot a deer grazing peacefully nearby. You excitedly grab your phone to take a closer picture, but your mom reminds you to stay a safe distance from wild animals.

You're at the park with your friend and see a dog by itself, tied to a bench and whimpering. The leash is really short and the dog can't reach the shade. It's a hot day!

You're at the park with your friend and their dog. The dog is playful and jumps up on you, knocking you over.

You go out one night to take out the garbage, and see two raccoons digging in the garbage can.

You're at the park playing when a dog you don't know runs up to you. You're not sure if it's friendly.

You're playing outside in the backyard when you realize your pet has disappeared! You call out their name, but there's no answer.

You're playing at your friend's house after school. Their hamster, Squeaks, is in a tiny cage with barely any bedding. Your friend picks Squeaks up roughly and squeezes it tightly, making Squeaks squeak loudly. You feel worried about Squeaks.

Your dog was in the backyard, but you suddenly hear a yelp and look out to see that there's another dog attacking your pet.

You're downstairs in the basement getting a snack when you hear a scurrying noise behind some boxes. You shine your flashlight and see a pair of beady eyes staring back.

You're playing frisbee in your backyard with your friend when the frisbee gets stuck high up in a tree. You see a beehive buzzing in the branches nearby. You want to get your frisbee back, but you're scared of getting stung.

You're walking on a nature trail with your friends when you see a snake slithering across the path in front of you. Some of your friends scream and jump back, but you remember what you learned about snakes in school. How can you act calmly and safely around a snake you encounter on a hike?

You're on a mountain hike with your family when you see a large bird soaring high above. It has a wingspan wider than you've ever seen before! You wonder what kind of bird it is, but you're not sure if it's safe to get your phone out to take a picture.

You're walking home from school and see a kitten stuck high up in a tree. It's crying and looks scared.

You're at the park with your friend when you see a group of older kids chasing pigeons. The pigeons seem scared and are flying erratically.

You don't think it's nice to chase the birds, but you're not sure what to say.

You're hiking in a nature trail and see a beautiful butterfly fluttering nearby. You want to catch it and take a closer look, but you know butterflies are delicate creatures.

You're walking along the beach with your family when you see a group of sea lions basking in the sun. You're excited to see them up close.

You're walking your dog on a leash in a crowded city park when you hear a loud noise that spooks your dog. The leash slips out of your hand, and your dog runs away! You're worried and don't know what to do in such a busy place.

You're on a school field trip to a petting zoo. You see a cute, fluffy goat and reach out to stroke its fur. Suddenly, the goat head-butts your hand! You're startled and a little afraid.

You're at the park playing on the swings when a friendly dog you don't know runs up and starts licking your face. You feel happy the dog likes you, but you're not sure if it's okay.

You're at a birthday party with pony rides. Everyone is taking turns riding, and it's your turn next. You're a little nervous because you've never ridden a horse before.

You're throwing a frisbee for your dog in the park when it accidentally lands near a group of unfamiliar dogs playing fetch. Your dog wants to join in, but you're unsure if it's safe.

Jennifer Tillock M.S. CCC-SLP

You're walking home from school when you see a tiny puppy shivering on the sidewalk. It looks lost and scared, but you're not sure if you should approach it.

You're playing in the back yard when you hear the gate creak open. You cautiously peek around the corner and see your neighbor's dog, a large and unfamiliar animal, wandering around your kitchen.

You're visiting a pet store with your parents and see a brightly colored parakeet in a cage. You reach your hand in to pet it, but the store employee warns you not to.

You're at the zoo and see a squirrel. You remember seeing someone feed the squirrels peanuts before. You take a peanut out of your lunchbox to give to the squirrel.

You're walking home from school and see a stray cat sitting on your porch. You want to pet it, but you don't know the cat.

You're building a sandcastle at the beach when you see a jellyfish washed up on the shore. It looks interesting, but you've heard they can sting.

You're at a friend's house and they have a horse. You want to ride it, but you've never ridden a horse before.

Medical

Body Smarts: Keeping Safe with Medicine and Medical Stuff!

Your body is amazing, and sometimes it needs a little extra help to stay healthy. That's where medicine comes in! But medicine can be tricky, so here are some super-important tips to be a Body Smarts whiz:

- **Never Take Mystery Meds:** Medicine bottles might look like juice boxes, but they're definitely not! Never take any medicine unless a trusted grown-up gives it to you and tells you what it is for.

- **Know Your Meds:** If you take medicine regularly, ask your grown-up about it. What is it for? How much do you take? This will make you a medicine master!

- **Supervised Swallowing:** Always swallow medicine with a grown-up watching. They can make sure you take the right amount and do it safely.

- **Choking Champions:** Be careful with small pills or capsules. If you have trouble swallowing them, ask a grown-up for help.

- **Stash and Trash:** Keep medicine bottles in a safe place, up high where little hands can't reach. When medicine is expired or you don't need it anymore, grown-ups will know how to throw it away safely.

- **Ouchie Ouch Alert:** If you ever bump yourself or scrape your knee, a grown-up can clean it and make you feel better. Don't put medicine on yourself without asking first!

- **Allergy Awareness:** If you have allergies, you might have special medicine like an inhaler. Talk to your grown-up about how and when to use it.

- **Doctor Detectives:** If you don't feel well, tell a grown-up! They can take you to the doctor, who is a special kind of detective who can help you feel better again.

By following these Body Smarts tips, you can be a medicine whiz and keep your body healthy and happy! Remember, your grown-ups are always there to help you feel safe and answer any questions you have about medicine or your health.

Scenarios

You fell off your bike and scraped your knee. You put a bandage on it, but a few days later it's red, swollen, and tender.

You're getting ready for bed and your mom gives you your medicine like usual. You take it without thinking, but then you realize it doesn't taste quite right.

You're having lunch with your friends and laughing while you eat. Suddenly, a piece of your sandwich gets stuck in your throat, and you can't breathe!

You're at the doctor's office with your mom. The doctor asks you some private questions about your health. You feel a little nervous answering them in front of your mom.

You've been giggling uncontrollably while playing with your friends, and now you can't stop hiccuping! They're getting annoying, but none of your silly tricks seem to work.

You're at the doctor's office with your mom. She starts explaining how you're feeling, but you know some of the details aren't quite right.

Your ears feel plugged up and muffled, making it hard to hear what the teacher is saying in class.

During recess, you're playing a game of tag with your friends, but everyone forgot their masks. You know it's important to wear them

at school, but you also don't want to miss out on playing. What do you do?

While lining up for lunch, you notice your mask keeps slipping down your nose. You're worried your classmates might see your face or that your teacher will get mad.

You're reading a book in class and having trouble breathing through your mask. It feels a little itchy too. You're worried about asking your teacher for a different mask in case they think you're complaining.

It's a hot and sunny day, and you're feeling sweaty during gym class. You want to take your mask off to cool down, but you know the rules about keeping them on while exercising indoors.

You're at the lunch table with your friends, and they're all making fun of someone for wearing a different kind of mask. It makes you feel uncomfortable, and you're worried they might make fun of yours next.

While walking home from school, you see a group of older kids not wearing masks and making fun of people who are. You feel scared and unsure of what to do if they approach you.

You're helping your parents unload groceries, and you notice they forgot to put their masks on before entering the store. You know it's important to follow the rules, but you don't want to embarrass them.

Jennifer Tillock M.S. CCC-SLP

You're at the dentist's office, and they ask you to wear a special mask while they work on your teeth. It looks different from your regular mask, and it makes you feel a little nervous.

It's picture day at school, and everyone is taking their masks off for the photos. You're a little worried about taking yours off, even for a short time.

You and your friend are playing together at the park, but they keep taking their mask off to talk or shout.

You're feeling under the weather and your mom gives you a spoonful of medicine. You take it without thinking, but then you remember it wasn't the bottle she usually gives you for your cold.

You're playing kickball at recess when your glasses go flying off your face during a run. You can't see very well without them, and you're worried you might step on them or lose them in the grass.

You're helping your mom bake cookies in the kitchen. You reach into the oven to grab the baking sheet, but accidentally brush your hand against the hot metal. It stings a lot, and your skin is red!

You're riding the bus home from school when you feel a giant sneeze coming on! You forgot to pack a tissue.

You were fooling around with friends and stuck a piece of candy up your nose. Now it is stuck and you can't blow it out.

You're helping your mom clean out the medicine cabinet, and you see two bottles that look almost identical. One is your allergy medicine, and the other is your mom's medication for headaches.

You're on a camping trip with your family and roasting marshmallows over the fire. A spark jumps up and lands in your eye! It stings a lot, and you're worried it might be hurt.

You're on the swings at recess when you feel a wave of nausea come over you. You think you might throw up! There's no trash can nearby, and you don't want to get your friends sick.

You're reading a book in class when you suddenly feel a warm trickle down your nose. Looking down, you see blood! You've gotten a nosebleed.

You are playing at recess and rub your eye, and now it is burning and watering.

You usually go to the nurse to get medicine every day at school. Today there is a substitute nurse, and your medicine bottle doesn't look the same.

You are in class when you remember your mom forgot to give you important medicine before you left for school.

You're playing tag at recess when you start to wheeze a little. You have asthma, and you usually carry your inhaler in your pocket, but you can't find it anywhere!

You're using scissors in class to cut paper for a project. Oops! You accidentally cut your hand and it starts to bleed.

You're at a friend's birthday party and they're serving delicious-looking peanut butter cookies. You know you have a peanut allergy, but the cookies look so good!

You're in gym class (PE) and suddenly feel dizzy or lightheaded like you might faint. The gym teacher isn't paying attention to you right now.

You're excited for pizza night with your family, but after eating a few slices, your stomach starts to feel achy and uncomfortable. You think you might have eaten too much too fast.

You're playing basketball at recess and accidentally rub your eye. Uh oh! You can't feel your contact lens anymore! You know it shouldn't be in your eye, but you're not sure where else to look.

You're halfway through your lunch and suddenly feel dizzy and lightheaded. You don't feel very hungry anymore.

You're playing tag on the playground when you trip and scrape your elbow. It stings a little, but there's no blood.

You're eating a delicious snack when you suddenly feel your throat getting itchy and your face getting puffy. You think you might be having an allergic reaction.

You're not feeling well, so your parent gives you a spoonful of medicine. But as you swallow, you realize it tastes different than the medicine you usually take.

You're cutting celery and accidentally cut your finger deeply. It's bleeding a lot and won't stop.

You're home alone and accidentally fall down the stairs. Your leg hurts really badly and you can't put any weight on it.

You're cutting carrots and accidentally cut your finger. There's a small cut, but it's only bleeding a little bit.

You're home alone with your younger brother. He trips and falls, hitting his head hard. He doesn't seem to be waking up.

You're home alone and accidentally take some of your mom's medicine. You weren't supposed to touch it.

You're in the cafeteria eating lunch when a piece of food gets stuck in your throat. You can't breathe!

You feel a sick feeling in your stomach and nausea rising. You think you might throw up.

You don't feel well. Your stomach hurts and you feel tired. You think you might need to see the school nurse.

You don't feel well. You're tired and achy, and all you want to do is crawl back into bed.

You wake up feeling sick and throw up at home before school starts.

Jennifer Tillock M.S. CCC-SLP

You're in class when your teacher suddenly stumbles and falls to the floor. They appear unconscious.

You're playing outside when a bee stings you on the arm. The sting site starts to swell up, and it hurts a lot.

You're spending all afternoon at the beach playing in the sun. Now, your skin is red, hot, and itchy.

You have an appointment with the doctor, but you're nervous about getting a shot.

You're prescribed medication for an illness, but you don't understand why you need to take it or how often.

You're playing tag on the playground and accidentally bump your head pretty hard. It hurts but there's no bleeding.

You're in class and get a bad stomachache that disrupts your focus. You're worried you might not make it to the bathroom on time.

You take your glasses off during gym class and can't find them when it's time to put them back on. You can't see very well without them.

You wake up feeling hot and achy. You suspect you might have a fever.

You ate something weird for lunch and now your tummy feels upset.

Social

Social Butterfly Squad: Spreading Kindness and Solving Problems Like a Pro!

Being social is like being a superhero – you get to connect with others, make friends, and have tons of fun! But sometimes, social situations can get a little tricky. Here are some super-secret tips to be a member of the Social Butterfly Squad and solve problems like a pro:

- **The "Kindness First" Rule:** Always treat others the way you want to be treated, with kindness and respect. A smile and a friendly hello can go a long way!

- **The "Word Wizard" Technique:** If someone says something unkind or hurts your feelings, use your words to tell them how you feel. For example, you could say "I don't like it when you call me names" or "Those words make me feel sad."

- **The "Body Language Buddy" System:** Words aren't the only way to communicate! Pay attention to body language like crossed arms or frowning, which might mean someone is unhappy.

- **The "Listen Up" Lesson:** Being a good friend means being a good listener. Let others share their thoughts and feelings, and show them you care by paying attention.

- **The "I" Message Mission:** When you need to solve a problem, use "I" messages to explain how a situation is making you feel. For example, "I feel left out when you don't include me in the game." This helps the other person understand your perspective.

- **The "Superhero Swap" Strategy:** Sometimes you might disagree with a friend. Instead of arguing, try to see things from their perspective. Imagine you're swapping superhero suits for a minute and see the problem from their eyes!

- **The "Walk Away Wonder" Option:** If someone is being unkind or disrespectful, it's okay to walk away. Tell them you're not interested in playing and find someone who wants to be kind.

- **The "Grown-Up Guidance Gang":** If you're ever feeling overwhelmed or stuck in a social situation, don't be afraid to ask a grown-up for help. They can be your partner in problem-solving and help you navigate any tricky social situations.

Remember: Everyone makes mistakes, and that's okay! By using these Social Butterfly Squad tips, you can build strong friendships, solve problems peacefully, and spread kindness wherever you go!

Jennifer Tillock M.S. CCC-SLP

Scenarios

Your table partner is sitting too close to you in class. You feel uncomfortable and crowded.

You're at your soccer game, starving after halftime. You head to the snack stand with your friends, but you only have a few dollars. Your friends all order hot dogs, but they cost more than you have.

You hear a rumor going around school about someone else. It might not be true, and you don't want to spread gossip.

You're waiting in line for a roller coaster ride with your friend, but they keep cutting in front of other people. You feel embarrassed and worried about getting in trouble.

A group of kids at school keeps calling you a silly nickname that you don't like. It makes you feel uncomfortable.

You're playing with building blocks with a friend at daycare, but they keep grabbing all the best pieces for themselves! You want to build a cool creation too

You watched a YouTube video before bed that talked about a scary monster. Now you can't stop worrying about it.

You made plans to play with a friend after school, but they never show up. You waited for a while and feel disappointed.

You and your sibling both want to watch different TV shows after dinner. You both feel strongly about your choices.

You're playing basketball at recess when someone accuses you of cheating. You didn't cheat, and you feel frustrated.

You and your best friend had a fight and aren't talking anymore. You miss them, but you're not sure who should apologize first.

You borrowed your friend's favorite toy at school and accidentally broke it. You're worried they'll be mad at you.

A family member keeps calling you a nickname you don't like, even after you've politely asked them to stop. How can you have a respectful conversation with your family member about how their words make you feel and suggest a different nickname you'd prefer?

You're watching a movie at the theater with some friends, and one of them keeps putting their arm around you even though you push it away gently.

It's your grandma's birthday party, and everyone is giving her hugs. You love your grandma, but you're not really a hugger. How can you show your love for your grandma in a different way that feels comfortable for you?

It's your birthday, and a classmate gives you a gift you don't like. You feel awkward and unsure how to react.

You forgot your lunch money at home, and your friend offers to buy you something. You feel bad about taking their money, but you're hungry.

You're at a school dance, but someone keeps asking you to dance even though you'd rather just chat with your friends.

A friend asks you to keep a secret about something they did that might get them in trouble. You don't feel comfortable lying, but you also don't want to get them in trouble.

You let your friend borrow your favorite pencil at school, but they don't return it when you ask. You need it back for classwork.

You're at the park with some classmates, but they're all playing a game you don't know how to play. You feel left out

A classmate tells you they like your new haircut, but they keep staring at it in a way that makes you feel self-conscious.

You're playing cards with a friend at lunch, and they want to trade cards. You know their card is much rarer than yours, but they pressure you to trade anyway.

You're at recess and see a friend playing with a cool new jump rope. You'd love to borrow it, but you're not sure if it's okay.

Your friend you chat with online says things that sometimes make you feel weird or uncomfortable.

You're invited to a party by some older kids, but you hear rumors they might be serving sugary drinks or snacks you're not supposed to have. You don't want to disappoint them, but you also don't want to break the rules or get sick.

You see someone in your class being unkind to another student. You feel bad for the person being targeted.

You and your best friend had a fight and aren't talking anymore. You miss them and want to make things right.

You're invited to a friend's birthday party, but you see another kid there that you don't get along with. You're worried about having a good time.

You're at the park with some older kids. They're playing a game that looks a little dangerous, and they pressure you to join in. You don't feel comfortable playing, but you don't want to seem like a scaredy-cat.

You're playing an online video game and you hear other players talking in a way that makes you uncomfortable.

You're having a sleepover with a friend, and they show you pictures on their phone that you know you shouldn't be looking at.

Jennifer Tillock M.S. CCC-SLP

You're at the movies with a friend. She really wants to see a superhero movie, but you'd prefer to see a spy movie.

You're hanging out with friends and someone tells a joke that makes you feel weird or embarrassed.

Your at a sleepover with your friend, and they want to watch a movie you are not interested in.

You're sitting at your usual lunch table, but your friends are all interested in a conversation you don't understand. You feel left out.

You're working on a group project with classmates, but they keep talking about things that aren't related to the project and gossiping about other kids.

You're playing basketball at recess, but the older kids keep making up new rules that favor them. It's not fair!

You're playing tag with friends, and one person keeps tagging you too hard, even though you've already been "out." It hurts a little, and you don't like it.

It's your turn to pick a game at playtime with friends, but everyone else wants to play something different. You feel frustrated because you never get to choose.

Your mom asks you to help clean the house, but you have a lot of homework that's due tomorrow.

Your brother ate your takeout from the fridge, even though it had your name on it. You're really upset!

You're spending the night at a friend's house. You're having fun playing games, but then something happens that makes you feel uncomfortable. You don't know how to tell your friend or your parents.

You're feeling really upset about something that happened earlier. You want some time alone to calm down before you talk about it.

Your class is working on a group project, but everyone is talking loudly and it's hard for you to concentrate.

You're at recess and your best friend isn't playing with you. They're playing with someone else, and you feel lonely.

A girl at lunch called you a name. It made you feel sad.

You're playing on the monkey bars at recess when a classmate playfully grabs you from behind in a way that makes you feel surprised and uncomfortable.

Your friend tells you a secret about themselves, but they make you promise not to tell anyone. You feel like you should tell a trusted adult if the secret involves something dangerous, but you don't want to break your promise.

Some friends were talking about something scary at lunch and now you can't stop worrying about it.

Internet/Social Media

Digital Detectives: Keeping Safe and Smart Online!

The internet is a vast and exciting world, full of information, games, and ways to connect with friends. But just like exploring a jungle, you need to be safe and know where to look! Here are some super-important tips to be a Digital Detective and have a fun and safe online adventure:

- **The "Secret Password Pact":** Just like your toothbrush, your passwords are personal! Don't share them with anyone except your grown-ups. Think of your password like a secret decoder ring for your online stuff.

- **The "Stranger Danger" Zone:** The internet can be a great way to connect with friends, but be careful about talking to strangers online. Don't give out personal information like your address or phone number to people you don't know in real life.

- **The "Think Before You Click" Challenge:** The internet is full of cool and funny things, but sometimes there might be things that aren't appropriate. If you see something that makes you feel uncomfortable, close the window and tell a grown-up.

- **The "Double-Check Download Detective":** Downloading games, apps, and movies can be fun, but only do it with a grown-up's permission. They can help you find safe and age-appropriate downloads.

- **The "Sharing Share-iously" Strategy:** Sharing online is fun, but be careful what you post. Don't share pictures or information about yourself or others without their permission. Once something is online, it can be hard to get rid of it.

- **The "Privacy Power Pact":** Many websites and apps have privacy settings. Talk to a grown-up about how to adjust them to keep your information safe.

- **The "Cyberbullying Stopper":** If you see someone being mean online, don't participate in it. Tell a grown-up or use the website's reporting tools. Remember, treat others online the way you want to be treated in real life!

- **The "Balance Beam Mission":** The internet is fun, but it's important to have a healthy balance. Set screen time limits with your grown-ups and make sure you spend time playing outside, reading, or doing other activities too!

- **The "Grown-Up Guidance Gang":** If you ever feel confused or unsure about something online, don't hesitate to ask a grown-up for help! They can be your partner in online safety and help you navigate the digital world.

By following these Digital Detective tips, you can explore the exciting world of the internet safely and have a ton of fun online! Remember, the internet is a powerful tool, and by using it responsibly, you can make it a positive and enriching experience.

Jennifer Tillock M.S. CCC-SLP

Scenarios

You're online looking at cat videos when an ad pops up with flashing lights and loud music. It has an inappropriate picture.

You see a picture of a celebrity online that's been edited to look a certain way. It makes you feel insecure about your own body. How can you challenge unrealistic beauty standards you see online and focus on healthy habits and feeling good about yourself on the inside and out?

Your friend is constantly on their phone and expects you to be available to chat all the time. You want to have some time to play offline or with other friends.

You see a funny meme online that you want to share with your friends, but it makes fun of a certain group of people. You're not sure if it's okay to share it.

You get a text message from an unknown number with a funny-looking link. Your friend tells you to click on it to see a hilarious video.

You get a friend request from someone you don't know, but they have a similar name to someone in your class. You're curious who it might be, but you're worried it could be a stranger.

You're chatting online with a friend about your favorite video game. They ask you for your home address so they can send you a care package.

You're chatting online with a friend you met on a gaming forum. They ask you for your last name to search for you on social media.

You've been chatting online with someone for a while, but you've never met them in person. They ask you to meet them at the park this weekend.

You're playing an online game when you get a message from someone who seems friendly. They offer you a free upgrade for your character if you click on a link and enter your username and password.

You game online with friends. Someone you don't know sends you a private message asking for your real name and address.

You and your friend are playing a game online that lets you share your high score on social media. Your friend wants to share their score, but you're worried they might accidentally share their personal information too.

You're playing a free game on your tablet and see a cool new outfit for your character. You want to buy it, but the game requires a password to make the purchase. You remember your older sibling's password.

You're browsing a website with cool toys and games. They have a special offer where you can win a free prize if you enter your parents' credit card information.

You're playing a new game online and it asks you to create an account with your username and password. You're not sure what information is safe to share.

You're excited about your weekend trip and want to share it with your friends online. You know it's not a good idea to share your home address or specific location. How can you share your trip photos and excitement while staying safe online?

You're filling out a profile on a kid-safe website. It asks for your birthday and your favorite color. What information is okay to share, and what shouldn't you give out?

You see someone posting mean comments about another kid in a school chatroom.

You're spending time online chatting with a friend, but they keep asking you personal questions that make you feel uncomfortable. You don't want to share that information.

You get a message online from someone you don't know. They're calling you names and making fun of you.

You're creating a new account for a cool online game, but you can't think of a strong password. Your friend suggests using their birthday.

You're playing an online game where you can chat with other players. Someone you don't know starts asking you personal questions about your family and where you live.

You receive a friend request from someone you don't know on a social media app. Their profile picture looks suspicious.

You see a funny meme online that you want to share with your friends, but it makes fun of someone else.

You find a website with a free game you want to download, but you're not sure if it's safe.

You're playing a new game and it asks you to allow access to your location and camera.

You're doing a school project about dinosaurs and you find a website with lots of information. How can you tell if the information is accurate and reliable before using it in your project?

You're following a cool new account on social media that posts funny videos. They start sending you private messages asking you personal questions and wanting to know your real name.

You promised your parents you'd only spend 30 minutes online, but you get caught up watching funny videos and lose track of time.

You're chatting with a friend online, but they keep asking you personal questions that make you feel uncomfortable. You don't want to share that information

You're in a chatroom talking to your friends. Everyone is typing really fast and using lots of abbreviations you don't understand. You feel left out.

Jennifer Tillock M.S. CCC-SLP

You receive a friend request on a social media app from someone you don't know. Their profile picture looks like a cartoon character. What are some red flags to look out for when accepting friend requests online, and how can you stay safe?

You're commenting on a YouTube video, but some of the other comments are rude and disrespectful.

You get a message online from someone you don't know. They're calling you names and making fun of you.

You're browsing the web and see a headline that sounds super interesting, like "OMG! You Won't Believe What This Cat Can Do!" You click on it, but instead of a cool cat video, you end up on a website with lots of flashing ads.

You're playing a game online when a pop-up window appears offering you free virtual currency for the game. You're tempted to click on it, but something seems suspicious.

You promised your parents you'd only spend 30 minutes online, but you get caught up watching funny videos and lose track of time.

You're playing a new app and it asks you to allow access to your location and camera. You're not sure why the app needs that information.

You find an awesome song online and want to share it with your friends by posting it on your social media page.

You're browsing the internet and find a cool website with free downloadable games. But before you can download anything, the website asks you to enter your email address and home address.

You see a friend post a picture of you online that you don't like. You feel embarrassed.

You find a website with a cool-looking game you want to download, but it requires installing software from an unknown source.

You're following a cool new account on social media that posts funny videos. They start sending you private messages asking you personal questions.

You're doing a school project about butterflies and you find a website with lots of information. How can you tell if the information is accurate?

You're excited about the new bike you got for your birthday and want to post a picture online. Your friend reminds you it's not a good idea to share your home address or location online. How can you share your excitement about your new bike safely online?

You're creating an account for a new online game, but you can't think of a strong password. What makes a good password, and how can you remember it?

You see a clickbait headline that says "Click Here to See the Cutest Kitten Ever!" You click on it, but instead of a cute kitten, you end up on a website with lots of confusing games and ads.

You're reading the comments section of a
funny online video, but some of the comments
are mean and hurtful.

Older Scenarios: 6th Grade& Up

Using the Scenarios (Teen)

Problem-Solving Through Guided Questions

The provided questions can be used in a variety of ways to guide teenagers through the problem-solving scenarios. Here's a breakdown of how each set of questions can be implemented:

Before You Start:

- **Think about your surroundings:** Ask the teenager to describe the setting of the scenario.
    - Who else is present? Are there adults nearby? Friends? Strangers?
    - Is it a familiar or unfamiliar environment?
- **Consider your safety:** What is the most important thing to ensure the teenager's safety in this situation?
    - Are there any immediate dangers they need to be aware of?
- **Identify your options:** Brainstorm a list of all the possible ways the teenager could react to the situation.
    - Encourage creative thinking and consider all possibilities, even seemingly unconventional ones.
- **Think about the consequences:** For each option identified, discuss the potential consequences.
    - What might be the positive and negative outcomes of each choice?

While Solving the Problem:

- **How can you use they use their resources?**
    - What tools or people can be helpful in this situation?
    - Does the teenager have a phone to call for help?
    - Are there adults they can approach for assistance?

- **What are their priorities?** What is most important to the teenager in this situation?
  - Is it their safety, their belongings, or something else?
- **Can the teen communicate effectively?**
  - How well can they clearly express their needs or concerns?
  - If they feel unsafe, how can they communicate that effectively?
  - If they need help, how can they ask for it politely and assertively?
- **How can they trust their gut?** Sometimes intuition can be a valuable tool.
  - Does something feel off about the situation?
  - Encourage the teenager to listen to their inner voice and act accordingly.

After Solving the Problem:

- **Did things go as planned?** If the situation was resolved successfully, discuss what worked well.
  - If things didn't go according to plan, explore what could have been done differently.
- **What did they learn from this experience?** Identify key takeaways from the scenario.
- **What skills or knowledge** can the teenager apply in future situations?
- **What could have been done to prevent** the problem in the first place?

Remember:

- **There are often multiple solutions to a problem.** The goal is to encourage critical thinking and discussion, not find a single "correct" answer.
- **Adapt the questions** to fit the specific scenario and the teenager's age and developmental level.
- **Use open-ended questions** that encourage discussion and elaboration.
- **Create a safe and supportive environment** where teenagers feel comfortable sharing their ideas and thought processes.

Visual Aids for Increased Understanding

There are several decision-making visuals that can be helpful for teenagers working through the scenarios in this book. Here are a few options:

Decision Matrix:

This is a grid with options listed on one axis and criteria (like safety, time, resources) on the other. Teenagers can assign a rating to each option based on how well it meets each criterion. This helps them see strengths and weaknesses of each choice at a glance.

Flowchart:

A flowchart is a visual representation of a decision-making process with a clear starting point and a defined outcome. It uses shapes and arrows to show different pathways based on choices made along the way. This can be helpful for situations with multiple steps or potential outcomes.

Pros and Cons List:

This is a simple but effective way to weigh the positive and negative aspects of each option. Listing pros and cons side-by-side allows teenagers to see the trade-offs involved in each choice.

Mind Map:

A mind map is a visual brainstorming tool that starts with a central question or problem and branches out to show associated ideas, solutions, and consequences. This can be helpful for exploring a wider range of possibilities and seeing how different factors might influence the decision.

Here are some additional tips for using visuals:

- **Keep it simple and clear.** The visual should be easy to understand and shouldn't add confusion.

- **Choose the right visual for the scenario.** Some scenarios might be better suited for a decision matrix, while others might benefit more from a flowchart.

- **Use visuals as a starting point for discussion.** Don't rely solely on the visual to make a decision. Use it to guide conversation and critical thinking.

- **Encourage teenagers to create their own visuals.** This can help them solidify their understanding of the problem and potential solutions.

By incorporating these decision-making visuals, you can provide teenagers with additional tools to analyze situations, weigh options, and make safe and effective choices.

Be Your Own School Superhero: Safety & Self-Advocacy Tips

School should be a safe and positive environment where you can learn, grow, and make lifelong memories. But mastering school life goes beyond academics – being a safety pro is key too! This guide will equip you with the knowledge and skills to navigate school like a superhero, focusing on both safety practices and self-advocacy techniques.

Be the Building Boss: Mastering Your Environment

Knowing your surroundings is crucial for staying safe in any situation. Here's how to become an expert on your school's layout:

- **Map It Out:** Early in the school year, take some time to map your school. Explore all the exits, classrooms, bathrooms, the cafeteria, the library, and the nurse's office. Mark down any specific safety features like fire extinguishers or AEDs (Automated External Defibrillators). Having a mental map of the school will help you navigate emergencies calmly and efficiently.

- **Know Your Exits:** Identify all the exits in your school building, including those near your classrooms and favorite hangouts. Don't rely on just one exit in case it's blocked during an emergency.

- **Plan Your Escape Route:** Once you know the exits, plan an escape route for each classroom you have throughout the day. Consider multiple escape options in case one route becomes obstructed.

Drill Dominator: Turning Practice into Preparedness

Fire drills, lock-down drills, and other emergency exercises might seem like interruptions, but they're vital for ensuring everyone's safety. Here's how to approach drills seriously:

- **Be Present, Be Prepared:** During drills, silence your phone and put away any distractions. Pay close attention to the instructions being given by teachers or administrators.

- **Follow the Rules:** Whether it's a fire drill requiring evacuation or a lockdown requiring silence, follow the instructions precisely. This ensures everyone can reach safety quickly and efficiently.

- **Ask Questions:** If you're unsure about any part of the drill, don't hesitate to ask your teacher or a school official for clarification. Understanding the purpose and procedures of each drill will make you feel more prepared in a real-life emergency.

Guarding Your Gear: Protecting Your Belongings

School backpacks, phones, lunchboxes, and gym bags hold your personal belongings. Here's how to keep them safe:

- **Lock It Up:** Utilize lockers or cubicles to store your belongings when not in use. Invest in a good lock for your locker and memorize the combination.

- **Keep it Close:** Don't leave your backpack unattended on the floor, under a desk, or hanging on a chair. Carry it with you whenever possible, especially in crowded areas.

- **Be Vigilant:** Keep an eye on your belongings throughout the day. Don't lend them to strangers, and report any suspicious activity to a teacher or another trusted adult.

- **Label Everything:** Label your belongings with your name and contact information. This increases the chances of getting them back if they're misplaced.

See Something, Say Something (And Mean It!)

Bullying, unsafe situations, or anything that makes you feel uncomfortable shouldn't be ignored. Here's how to be a voice for yourself and others:

- **Be an Upstander, Not a Bystander:** Witnessing bullying or any form of harassment? Don't stay silent. Speak up in a safe way, or report it to a trusted adult like a teacher, counselor, or administrator.

- **Details Matter:** When reporting an incident, provide as much detail as possible. This could include the location, the people involved, and what specifically happened.

- **Empower Others:** If you see someone else being targeted or feeling unsafe, encourage them to speak up or offer to report the incident along with them. There's strength in numbers.

Crossing the Street Like a Champion: Mastering Traffic Safety

Getting to and from school safely is just as important as what happens inside the building. Here are some tips for navigating streets and sidewalks:

- **Crosswalk Champion:** Cross streets only at designated crosswalks, never in the middle of the block. Always look both ways before crossing, even at crosswalks, and wait for the "walk" signal if one is present.

- **Sidewalk Superhero:** Sidewalks are your designated walking area. Avoid walking in the street, especially near traffic. If there are no sidewalks, walk facing oncoming traffic and be extra cautious.

- **Be Alert, Not Distracted:** When walking to or from school, put away your phone and other distractions. Pay attention to your surroundings and focus on the path ahead.

Kindness Crew Captain: Building a Positive School Environment

School should be a place where everyone feels welcome and respected. Here's how to be part of a positive and inclusive environment:

- **Kindness Contagion:** Treat everyone with respect, from your classmates and teachers to the cafeteria staff and janitors. Remember, words and actions have power. Choose kindness and inclusivity to create a positive school environment for everyone.

- **Embrace Differences:** Celebrate the diversity of your school community. Everyone comes from different backgrounds and has different experiences. Embrace these differences and learn from each other.

- **Stand Up to Bullying:** If you see someone being bullied, don't be a bystander. Be an upstander! Offer support to the person being targeted, and report the incident to a trusted adult.

Online Safety Squad Leader: Navigating the Digital World

Technology is a big part of our lives, but it's important to be safe online just as you are offline. Here are some tips to be a leader in online safety:

- **Surf Smart:** When using school computers or tablets, be mindful of the websites you visit. Stick to school-approved websites and avoid accessing anything inappropriate or distracting.

- **Privacy Power:** Don't share personal information online, such as your address, phone number, or birthdate. Be cautious about what you post on social media, as once something is online, it can be difficult to delete.

- **Stranger Danger (Online Too!):** Just like in the real world, be wary of interacting with strangers online. Don't accept friend requests from people you don't know, and avoid sharing personal information in chatrooms or online games.

- **Cyberbullying Awareness:** Cyberbullying can be just as hurtful as traditional bullying. If you experience cyberbullying, don't respond back. Report the incident to a trusted adult and consider blocking the person who is harassing you online.

Don't Be Shy, Speak Up!: Advocating for Your Well-Being

Feeling unwell or uncomfortable in class? Don't hesitate to speak up! Here's how to advocate for yourself:

- **Your Health Matters:** If you're feeling sick, have a headache, or need to use the restroom, don't be afraid to ask your teacher for permission. Your health and well-being are important for learning effectively.

- **Clarify Confusion:** Didn't understand a lesson or need clarification on an assignment? Don't suffer in silence. Ask your teacher for help after class, during office hours, or send a polite email with your questions.

- **Learning Differences:** Do you have a learning difference like dyslexia or ADHD? Let your teachers and school counselor know. This way, you can receive the support and accommodations you need to succeed in school.

Be Prepared, Be a Hero: Having a Mini First-Aid Kit

Being prepared for minor accidents can be a lifesaver. Here's how to create a mini first-aid kit to keep in your backpack:

- **Pack the Essentials:** Include basic supplies like bandages in various sizes, antiseptic wipes, pain relievers (if allowed by school policy), and a small pair of scissors.

- **Know What's In It:** Review the contents of your first-aid kit with a parent or guardian and learn how to use each item safely.

- **Be a Helping Hand:** Your first-aid kit can also be helpful to others. If you see someone with a scrape or a minor injury, offer to help them clean and bandage it using the supplies in your kit.

Talk to Your Team: Communication with Parents/Guardians

Open communication with your parents or guardians is vital for your safety and well-being at school. Here's how to stay connected:

- **Daily Debrief:** Have a brief chat with your parents or caregivers about your day at school. Share any concerns you might have about safety, bullying, or academic challenges.

- **Listen and Learn:** Pay attention to any safety advice your parents or guardians share with you. They want you to be safe and might have valuable insights about your school or neighborhood.

- **Work Together:** If you experience an issue at school, such as feeling bullied or having difficulty understanding an assignment, talk to your parents or guardians. They can help you advocate for yourself or reach out to school officials for support.

Remember: By following these safety and self-advocacy tips, you're well on your way to becoming a school safety superhero! You have the power to create a positive and safe learning environment for yourself and others. Don't be afraid to speak up, ask for help, and embrace your inner hero!

Scenarios

You're engrossed in a complex biology lesson when an insistent urge to use the restroom disrupts your concentration. You know it might disrupt the class and you're worried about missing key information during your absence.

Every time you visit your locker to grab your gym clothes, you notice a guy lingering nearby, staring intently at you. This unwanted attention makes you feel increasingly uneasy and unsafe.

The combination you've used for months to unlock your locker suddenly fails. You juggle your books and frustration as you're locked out of your belongings, potentially including your lunch and classwork.

Your history teacher announces a missing assignment, and your heart sinks. You distinctly remember turning it in with the rest of the class, but dread washes over you as you contemplate potential consequences.

Disbelief clouds your mind as you stare at the grade scrawled on your meticulously researched science project. It's significantly lower than you expected, and the feedback seems harsh and confusing.

In the middle of furiously taking notes during chemistry class, your school-issued tablet sputters and dies. Panic surges as attempts to power it back on prove futile, leaving you scrambling to catch up.

It's finally Friday night, and you settle in to tackle your weekend homework assignment. But as you reach for your tablet, dread sets in - a dead battery and a missing charger throw a wrench into your plans.

You disagree with a group project idea at school. Anxious about speaking up, you strategize how to voice your opinion constructively and propose an alternative solution.

You rush to your locker between classes, needing to grab your science textbook for the upcoming lab. But as you approach, you find two friends engrossed in a conversation, completely blocking access.

You scan the math test in front of you, filled with problems that resemble nothing you've practiced in class. Confusion clouds your mind, leaving you unsure of how to proceed or even where to begin.

You power on your laptop to start your history research paper, but instead of the familiar desktop, you're greeted with a glitching mess of distorted colors and cryptic error messages. The device seems unusable.

During a crowded school assembly, you spot a bulge in someone's pocket. The unmistakable shape of a gun sends a jolt of terror through you. Unsure of how to react, you're frozen in a moment of fear.

Seated in Spanish class, your teacher launches into a rapid-fire lecture, her words blurring together at a dizzying pace. You struggle to keep up, feeling lost and discouraged in the fast-moving lesson.

The usual bus stop whizzes by in a blur, leaving you stranded on the sidewalk. Confusion mixes with worry as you realize the school bus didn't stop for you, and you're late for your first class.

Your math teacher meticulously explains a new concept in Algebra, but despite nodding along, a fog of confusion lingers in your mind. You have no idea how to solve the looming practice problems.

You've finished your meticulously crafted English essay and eagerly submit it online. But the website throws you a curve ball, refusing to accept your work due to a technical glitch. Frustration mounts as you grapple with the unexpected hurdle.

Your car unexpectedly sputters to a halt on the way to school. Forced to borrow a friend's vehicle, you arrive at school only to face a new challenge: the parking lot requires a permit you don't have.

You stare at the daunting essay prompt for your literature class, your mind a jumble of thoughts. You're unsure exactly what your teacher wants you to write about, leaving you feeling paralyzed and unsure how to proceed.

A piercing fire alarm shatters the peaceful silence of the library. Confusion fills the room as everyone jumps up, unsure of the situation and how to proceed safely.

Lunchtime arrives and you head towards the cafeteria to meet your friends. But amid the sea of unfamiliar faces, you realize you're lost and separated from your group. Panic rises as you navigate the crowded lunchroom alone.

You eagerly open your lunch tray, ready to devour your favorite meal. But instead, you find an unfamiliar dish you've never seen before. You remember having a food allergy, but the ingredients are a mystery.

Walking down the hallway between classes, a group of students stops you and starts making fun of your clothes. Feeling belittled and unsafe, you know you need to do something to address the situation.

During a high-stakes chemistry test, you witness a blatant case of cheating. A student blatantly copies answers from their neighbor, and you're caught in a moral dilemma, unsure if you should speak up and risk causing a scene.

You're participating in a class online forum when a discussion turns hostile. Offensive language erupts from another student.

Dizziness and nausea creep over you unexpectedly in the middle of English class. You try to focus on the ongoing lecture, but your worsening condition makes you suspect you might be getting sick. Do you tough it out or risk disrupting the class to seek help?

Jennifer Tillock M.S. CCC-SLP

You meticulously pack your backpack the night before, ensuring you have everything you need for the upcoming school day. But upon arriving at your first class, you reach for your textbook and discover it's vanished from both your bag and locker. Panic rises as you contemplate the day ahead without your crucial study materials.

The day of your history presentation arrives, and your stomach churns with nervousness. You practiced your speech countless times, but self-doubt creeps in, leaving you worried you might forget everything in front of the class.

You're working diligently on a group project with a partner assigned by the teacher. However, your teammate isn't pulling their weight, leaving you to shoulder most of the work. The deadline looms, and you worry about your grade suffering due to their lack of effort.

Relief washes over you as you locate your favorite jacket in the lost and found. But as you pick it up, a wave of disappointment hits you - the jacket has been ripped and stained, seemingly beyond repair.

You carefully choose your outfit for school, following the dress code guidelines as best you understand them. However, upon entering the school building, you notice another student being pulled aside by an administrator for a dress code violation. Uncertainty clouds your mind - are you also at risk of being sent home for non-compliance?

Gym class approaches, and your anxiety spikes. Due to physical limitations, you struggle to participate in certain activities. You don't want to draw attention to yourself, but you also don't want to risk failing the class due to missed participation points.

The class eagerly prepares for a much-anticipated field trip. However, you realize you forgot to get the permission slip signed by your parent. Panic sets in as you contemplate whether you'll be allowed to participate in the trip without it.

During a crucial biology exam, you accidentally mark the wrong answer sheet. Realizing your mistake just moments after submitting your test, you're filled with dread and unsure if there's anything you can do to rectify the situation.

The lunch line snakes forward, and your stomach growls for its usual lunchtime treat. Finally, you reach the front, only to witness a group of students nonchalantly toss their barely touched lunches into the overflowing trash. A wave of guilt washes over you – such a waste!

As a new student, you navigate the unfamiliar school building, desperately trying to find your locker before your first class. Anxiety rises as minutes tick by, and you realize you're hopelessly lost and potentially late.

An awkward silence fills the classroom after the teacher cracks a joke that lands flat, leaving some students visibly uncomfortable. Unsure if the teacher is aware of the awkward tension, you contemplate speaking up to acknowledge it or letting it pass.

You're presenting your science project to the class, relying on a software program to display your visuals and data. But when you launch the program, it crashes unexpectedly, leaving you scrambling to present your findings without the aid of your prepared materials.

During a particularly grueling gym class session, you feel increasingly overheated and dizzy. Pushing yourself to keep up with the exercises seems risky, but you don't want to appear weak by sitting out.

A test question appears on your English exam that you find deeply uncomfortable and irrelevant to the class material. It seems to target a personal experience you'd rather not discuss publicly. You're unsure if it's appropriate to question the validity of the question with the teacher.

College application deadlines loom on the horizon, but you feel overwhelmed and unsure where to begin the process. You have limited guidance or support at home, leaving you scrambling to navigate financial aid applications, deadlines, and school selection.

A loud fight erupts in the lunchroom, drawing a crowd of curious onlookers. You feel unsafe caught in the middle of the chaos, unsure of how to react or where to seek help.

A substitute teacher arrives for your English class completely unprepared, lacking clear instructions or lesson plans. The class descends into confusion as valuable learning time seems to be wasted. Do you speak up about the situation or simply wait for the regular teacher to return?

On a crowded field trip with your class, you get separated from your classmates amid the excitement of exploring the new location. Panic sets in as you realize you're lost and alone in an unfamiliar environment.

During locker room activities after gym class, you witness inappropriate behavior from some of your classmates. The situation makes you feel unsafe and uncomfortable, but you're unsure how to address the issue without causing a scene.

College seems far off, but rumors swirl among the upperclassmen about college prep expectations and rigorous workloads. Feeling overwhelmed by the unknown, you don't know where to begin preparing for the challenges that lie ahead.

Your heart races as you enter the restroom, only to find a bigger student blocking the exit. He demands your lunch money, his menacing tone leaving no doubt about his seriousness.

The fire alarm blares, but Michael cowers under his desk, overwhelmed by the noise. You know it's crucial to evacuate, but also see the fear paralyzing him.

Panic claws at you - your lucky charm necklace is missing! A glimmer of hope emerges in the lost and found, but it hangs with another name attached. Taking it feels wrong, but you can't bear to lose it.

The lunch line snakes forward, and your stomach growls for your favorite pizza. But as you reach the counter, the lunch monitor waves your friend in front of you, grabbing the last slice and leaving you with disappointment.

You watch in horror as a group of kids climb a precarious structure on the playground. One wrong move could send them tumbling, and you're unsure if you should intervene or alert a supervisor.

You spent hours researching and creating your group project presentation, only to have your partner present it alone, taking all the praise without acknowledging your contributions.

Your vision blurs and dizziness washes over you mid-class, symptoms of your anxiety disorder. But the teacher mistakes it for goofing off and threatens detention.

Test day arrives, and your palms sweat as you stare at the confusing questions. Your dyslexia makes processing the information a struggle, but you haven't confided in your teacher about your learning disability.

A text notification pops up - you accidentally sent the upcoming school play's surprise ending to a classmate who isn't in the cast. Now the secret might be out!

The teacher excitedly explains a new science project, but her rapid speech and technical terms leave you lost. You're surrounded by classmates nodding along, but you have no idea what to do.

You join the robotics club, excited to build cool machines. But lately, the older members constantly put down your ideas and make fun

of your mistakes. You feel increasingly unwelcome and unsure if you should stay.

Every day on the bus ride home, a group of students yell insults and make fun of your clothes. You feel targeted and unsafe, but don't know who to tell.

During a pop quiz, your friend nudges you and whispers to copy their answers. You know cheating is wrong, but your friend keeps pressuring you, making you feel anxious and unsure what to do.

Walking down the hallway, you spot a small, unlabeled container with a strange, chemical smell. You're unsure what it is and worried it might be dangerous.

Lunchtime descends into chaos as a food fight erupts. Trays fly, ketchup splatters, and students slip on spilled food. You fear getting hurt or caught in the crossfire.

Mr. Jones' face turns red as he accuses the class of cheating on a surprise quiz. You know everyone played fair, and the anger in his voice makes you feel nervous and unsure how to respond.

Your heart sinks as you realize your favorite library book is missing from your backpack. You remember checking it out weeks ago, and dread the potential late fees and trouble you might face.

Excitement for the class field trip to the museum bubbles over, but as you board the bus, panic sets in. You forgot to bring the permission slip your parents signed, and worry you might be left behind.

During a crowded science experiment, a classmate repeatedly bumps into you from behind, giggling with their friends. The contact feels unnecessary and makes you feel increasingly uncomfortable.

Rushing down the hallway between classes, you witness a student collapse to the ground, their body convulsing uncontrollably. Fear paralyzes you for a moment. The situation demands immediate action. Do you call for help or attempt to intervene yourself, even if you've never witnessed a seizure before?

The substitute teacher assigns an overwhelming amount of homework, an entire week's workload crammed into a single night. Knowing the impossibility, you're unsure if voicing your concerns or suffering in silence is the better course of action.

The fire alarm shrieks, and during the evacuation, you discover a forgotten lighter in your bag. Panic sets in as you decide - discreetly dispose of it yourself or inform a teacher about the potential fire hazard.

You witness your friend being ostracized by their group project partners, deliberately excluded from discussions and ignored. Their frustration is evident, but you fear stirring the pot.

The sub throws an impossible homework load at the class - a week's worth in one night! Knowing it's unreasonable, do you voice your concerns or suffer in silence?

Your friend is being ostracized by their group project partners, deliberately excluded from discussions. Their frustration is clear, but you worry about stirring the pot. Do you speak up for them or avoid potential conflict?

Excitement bubbles over as your class prepares to embark on a much-anticipated field trip to the zoo. But as you board the bus, dread creeps in. You realize you left the permission slip signed by your parents at home.

Jennifer Tillock M.S. CCC-SLP

Kitchen

Become a Kitchen Master: Safety & Confidence in the Kitchen!

The kitchen is more than just a place to grab snacks – it's your zone to unleash your inner chef! But before you whip up a culinary masterpiece, mastering some safety skills and knowing how to speak up for yourself are key ingredients.

Safety Superstar:

- **Heat It Up Safely:** Always use pot holders when handling hot pots and pans. Don't leave hot items unattended on the stove, and turn off burners when you're done.

- **Sharp Stuff Alert:** Sharp knives are awesome tools, but use them with caution! Keep them pointed downwards and cut away from your body. Ask for help if you're unsure about using a sharp tool.

- **Fire Safety First:** Keep flammable objects away from the stove top. If a small grease fire occurs, don't panic! Turn off the heat, cover the pan with a lid or dump baking soda on it, and tell an adult immediately. Do not use water on a grease fire!

- **Stop Food-borne Illness:** Wash your hands thoroughly with soap and warm water before handling food and after handling raw meat. Pay attention to expiration dates and store leftovers properly. Clean surfaces and utensils that come into contact with food to prevent the spread of bacteria.

- **Appliance Awareness:** Get familiar with how appliances like ovens and microwaves work. Never attempt to use a broken appliance, and always unplug them before cleaning.

- **Know Your Limits:** Don't attempt recipes that are too complex for your skill level. It's better to start simpler and build your confidence gradually.

- **Prevent Cross-Contamination:** Use separate cutting boards for raw meat and produce. This prevents bacteria from raw meat from contaminating your vegetables and fruits.

- **Wash your hands thoroughly** and clean surfaces with soapy water in between handling different ingredients, especially after touching raw meat.

- **Thawing Smarts:** Never thaw frozen meat on the counter at room temperature. Thaw it in the refrigerator, in cold water, or using the defrost setting on the microwave.

- **Beware of Burns:** Be cautious of steam when lifting pot lids. Tilt the lid away from yourself to avoid accidental burns.

- **Sharp Object Disposal:** Don't throw sharp objects like knives or broken glass in the trash can. Wrap them securely in newspaper or cardboard before discarding them.

- **Loose Clothing Caution:** Avoid wearing loose clothing or dangling jewelry while cooking, as they can easily catch fire or get caught in appliances.

- **Foot Traffic Flow:** Be mindful of others in the kitchen. Keep walkways clear and avoid blocking access to appliances or cabinets.

Self-Advocacy Savvy:

- **Don't Be Shy, Ask Away!** Recipes can be tricky, and sometimes you don't know how to use an appliance. Don't be afraid to ask for help or clarification from a parent or guardian if you're unsure about a step.

- **Feeling the Heat?** The kitchen can get hot! If you're feeling overwhelmed or uncomfortable, speak up and take a break. Your well-being is important!

- **Food Allergies or Preferences?** Let whoever's in charge of the meal know about any allergies or dietary restrictions you have. There are always ways to modify dishes to ensure everyone enjoys the meal safely.

- **Kitchen Collaboration:** Cooking with friends or family can be fun! Discuss tasks and responsibilities beforehand to avoid confusion or frustration.

- **Respect the Cleanup Crew:** Nobody enjoys a messy kitchen! Offer to help with cleaning up after cooking. It shows responsibility and appreciation for the shared space.

Bonus Tip: Feeling adventurous in the kitchen? Research a new recipe you'd like to try and present it to your family or guardian as the main course for a meal. It's a great way to showcase your newfound skills and confidence!

By following these tips, you'll be well on your way to becoming a confident and safe kitchen master! Now go forth and create delicious culinary memories!

Scenarios

You fling open the fridge, ready for a refreshing snack. But instead of cool air, a wave of heat blasts you. Panic rises as you realize all the food is warm. The power must be out!

You're helping bake cookies with your younger sibling. They're super excited and want to dump all the ingredients into the bowl at once. Flour goes everywhere, spilling onto the counter and even landing on the floor! The kitchen is a mess, and it's hard to navigate around the flour to grab other ingredients.

The sizzle of bacon fills the air, promising a delicious breakfast. But the delightful sound is soon replaced by the blaring shriek of the smoke alarm. Burnt bacon and a smoky kitchen await.

You're helping your friend bake cookies. You grab a bag of flour from the cabinet, but your friend needs to use the mixer right behind you. Oops!

The aroma of golden brown cookies fills your senses, but reaching into the oven is impossible. You search frantically, but your oven mitt is missing! Retrieving those delicious treats becomes a challenge.

You're grabbing a juice box from the fridge after soccer practice. The fridge door is swinging open a bit, and you see your parent trying to reach a pot in the back.

You're cooking dinner by yourself and accidentally set off the smoke alarm. The alarm is blaring, but the fire seems small and contained. Torn between leaving the house and trying to extinguish it yourself, you weigh the risks.

You're experimenting with a new recipe in the kitchen when the oil in a pan ignites. Startled and unsure how to react, you must make a quick decision to extinguish the flames safely or evacuate the house for help.

You're doing laundry and notice the dryer vent hose is disconnected. Lint has built up around the opening, and you're worried it might be a fire hazard.

You're helping your sibling with a science project that involves using household chemicals. The instructions seem a little unclear, and you're worried about mixing the wrong things together.

You're feeling overwhelmed with chores and homework. You consider putting it all off until later, but you know you'll just be more stressed tomorrow.

You're taking out the trash and see a stray dog rummaging through the bags. The dog appears aggressive, and you're unsure how to approach the situation.

You're relaxing in your room when you hear a strange noise coming from outside your window. It sounds like someone might be trying to break in, and you're home alone.

You're leaving the house for a sleepover and realize you forgot your charger. You ask your parent if you can borrow theirs, but they need it for work tomorrow.

Spaghetti night seems perfect - until you spot the bulging lid on the can. Is it safe to eat? The uncertainty throws your dinner plans into a tizzy.

You're making a sandwich in the kitchen while your sibling unloads the dishwasher. You spread mayo on your bread, but the mayo jar is right in front of the cabinet door they need to open.

Confidently, you grab a cutting board to prep the chicken for tonight's dinner. But a horrifying realization dawns: you used that same board for raw vegetables earlier! Cross-contamination fears cloud your plans.

Looking down, you see your pet dog's leash trailing across the floor, forgotten from earlier when you came in. Dazed for a moment, you gather yourself up, glad you weren't seriously hurt.

You hit the toaster button for your morning bagel, eager for a satisfying pop. But instead, smoke billows out and sparks fly. Triumph turns to terror as you witness a toaster malfunction.

You made all the burger patties, now you need to chop the tomato and onion. You grab them

and start chopping them without washing your hands with soap.

You're rushing to grab a glass of milk after a hot soccer game. You open the fridge, one hand fumbling in the back for the milk carton. Suddenly, your foot catches on something soft. The kitchen rug is wrinkled up.

You are chopping up a salad when you sneeze, right into the bowl.

Cracking an egg for breakfast, a pungent odor assaults your senses - it's definitely rotten!

Disaster strikes! A glass shatters on the floor, leaving you barefoot in a mess of scattered shards.

Feeling like a culinary rockstar, you are wearing a really cute blouse with flowing sleeve. But it's your turn to cook.

A forgotten lasagna lurks in the fridge. Hunger pangs tempt you, but you can't remember how long it's been there.

Disappointment strikes! You reach for a doughnut, but to discover a gaping hole in the packaging. A sneaky critter enjoyed a snack, it seems.

The delicious lunch sandwich leaves a horrifying aftertaste. After looking at it, you find the bread was covered in mold!

Zapping popcorn for movie night, the microwave fills the air with a scary sparking and crackling.

Jennifer Tillock M.S. CCC-SLP

Pasta night turns into a boiling nightmare! Your pot overflows with starchy water, threatening to flood the stovetop.

Sizzling and spitting, a pan fire erupts while you're frying dinner!

Your perfectly olden toast seems to be playing hide-and-seek. Stuck in the toaster, it refuses to pop up. You need to carefully retrieve it without burning yourself.

Whipping up a stir-fry, a rogue sneeze sends a cloud of chili powder flying – right into your eyes!

Lost in your phone, you leave a pot of water boiling on the stove. The water evaporates, and the pot starts smoking and makes a scary burning smell.

Reaching for a knife in a cluttered drawer, you accidentally grab it by the blade and cut your finger.

Taking a frozen pizza out of the freezer, you accidentally drop it on the floor. The box breaks open, and the pizza isn't as solid as you thought.

You're deep-frying some delicious food, but the basket overflows and hot oil splatters everywhere, including the stovetop.

You're cutting up raw chicken breast and vegetables for dinner and realize you only have one cutting board.

You preheat the oven for some cookies, but forget you left a plastic spatula inside. The plastic melts, triggering the smoke alarm.

Cleaning up after dinner, you accidentally knock a fork into the garbage disposal while it's running.

You're following a recipe that calls for grating cheese. You reach for the box grater a little too quickly and scrape your knuckles.

Reaching for a jar of cookies on a high shelf, the jar slips, sending cookies flying and shattering glass on the counter.

Digging in the back of the fridge for a leftover, a carton of milk explodes, soaking everything in its path.

Whipping up a smoothie, you forget to secure the lid properly. As you blend, the mixture explodes, spraying fruit and liquid everywhere.

Washing a sharp knife and distracted by your phone, the knife slips and falls into the sink, splashing water everywhere.

Reheating leftovers in a metal container in the microwave, sparks fly and the microwave makes a loud buzzing noise.

Feeling adventurous, you try to broil some steak for the first time. You forget to set the timer and the steak burns to a crisp.

Jamming out to music while making dinner, you bump into a chair, sending a pot of boiling water teetering on the edge of the stove.

You're multitasking in the kitchen, boiling pasta on one burner and frying chicken on another. You forget about the chicken and it smokes up the whole kitchen.

Your friend is coming over to dinner and you can't remember if she was allergic to peanuts or strawberries, and you really wanted to make stir-fry with peanuts and strawberry shortcake.

In the middle of lunch, a mild allergic reaction hits from an unexpected ingredient in your food. You need to discreetly alert an adult without causing a scene.

Grocery bags overflow like a volcano, threatening to spill their contents. Hours fly by unnoticed, and raw chicken sits at room temperature on the counter. Dinnertime approaches.

The steak looks like a masterpiece - beautifully seared on the outside. But a peek inside reveals a shocking truth - a raw, pink center. It smells good.

Morning arrives, and you reach blindly for the familiar orange juice carton. But instead of a refreshing drink, a burning sensation erupts in your mouth! A quick glance reveals a horrifying mistake. What cleaning product disguised itself as breakfast?

Your trusty blender sputters and coughs, sparks flying like mini fireworks. Smoke fills the air, replacing the usual whirring sound. Your morning smoothie dreams are dashed.

Lost in a world of suds, you scrub away at the dirty dishes. Suddenly, the floor feels different – slippery and treacherous.

Lasagna night is here! You lift the steaming pot from the oven, eager to impress your family. But your grip weakens, and the pot wobbles precariously.

Chopping time! In a rush, you toss your knives into a drawer like puzzle pieces. Reaching in later, you grab the wrong end - sharp metal instead of a smooth handle.

The recipe video is captivating! Each step appears effortless on your phone screen. But your focus on the digital world makes you oblivious to the real world.

Jennifer Tillock M.S. CCC-SLP

Bathroom

Be a Bathroom Boss: Safety Superstar Edition!

The bathroom isn't just for brushing your teeth – it's your zone for relaxation and self-care. But before you unwind, mastering some safety skills and knowing how to speak up for yourself are key!

Safety Superstar:

- **Shower Power:** Keep the floor dry! Use a bath mat with a non-slip backing to prevent slips. Avoid using electronic devices like phones or shavers in the shower to prevent electrical shocks.

- **Hot Stuff Alert:** Test the water temperature before stepping in with your hand or foot, not directly with any body part. Avoid scalding hot water – adjust the knobs gradually for a comfortable shower. Consider installing a safety valve to prevent excessively hot water.

- **Sharp Objects Stash:** Put razors and other sharp objects in a secure container with a lid after use. Avoid leaving them on the edge of the sink or shower where they could fall and cause cuts. Consider using a wall-mounted razor holder for easy access and storage.

- **Bathroom Buddy System:** If you have any medical conditions that might put you at risk in the bathroom, consider letting someone know you're showering, especially if you live alone. This could be a parent, roommate, or trusted neighbor.

- **First-Aid Friend:** Keep a small first-aid kit stocked with bandages, antiseptic wipes, and any other necessary medications in an easily accessible cabinet in the bathroom for minor cuts, scrapes, or allergic reactions.

- **Light Fantastic:** Ensure proper lighting in the bathroom to avoid tripping hazards from poorly lit areas.

- **Cleanliness Counts:** Regularly clean and disinfect surfaces like countertops, sinks, and shower areas to prevent the spread of germs.

- **Medication Management:** Store all medications in their original containers and out of reach of children and pets. Never share medications with others.

- **Air it Out:** Open a window or use the bathroom fan after showering to prevent mold and mildew growth.

Self-Advocacy Savvy:

- **Privacy Matters:** Knock before entering a bathroom that's occupied, and close the door behind you when using it. Respect everyone's need for privacy.

- **Feeling Unwell?** Don't be shy! If you're not feeling well or need something while in the bathroom, speak up and ask for help from a parent, guardian, or trusted adult.

- **Sharing is Not Always Caring:** Don't share personal hygiene products like razors or towels to avoid spreading germs.

- **Temperature Talk:** If the bathroom gets too hot or stuffy, let someone know so they can adjust the ventilation or open a window.

- **Shower Space Sharing:** Communicate with siblings or roommates about shower schedules to avoid conflicts or long waits.

Bonus Tip: Feeling stressed? Take advantage of that relaxing shower time! Play some calming music, light a scented candle (with adult supervision!), or practice some deep breathing exercises to de-stress and recharge.

By following these tips, you'll be well on your way to becoming a confident and safe bathroom boss! Now go forth and have a self-care spa day (well, at least a relaxing shower)!

Scenarios

You take a long, hot shower and step out feeling refreshed. However, the bathroom is filled with steam and a musty odor.

You were taking a relaxing bubble bath while reading your Kindle. You set it down for a second, but accidentally elbow it and it falls in the tub.

You want to take a bath and listen to the radio, but your bathroom is small and only place to put it is on the edge of the bathtub.

You want to use the iron to give your hair some nice curls. When you go to plug it in, you notice the wires are poking out of the cord.

You are drawing a nice, relaxing bubble bath, but leave the bathroom to answer the phone. When you get back, the water is falling onto the floor.

While taking a shower, you notice a large patch of mold growing in the corner, and the shower is smelly.

You decided to dye your hair. You've had the dye on for several minutes when it begins to burn badly.

You reach for your razor after shaving your legs, but notice your sibling has used it without replacing the blade.

You hear a noise at the door while showering at home and suspect someone might be trying to enter.

You're mid-blowout, feeling like a hair-flipping pro, when disaster strikes. A rogue strand gets yanked right into the back of the dryer with a terrifying whoosh! Panic sets in – is your hair permanently attached to the machine?

You proudly wield your cleaning spray, tackling grime in the bathroom. But with each spritz, a nauseating odor fills the air. Your head starts to spin – is this intense cleaning session worth the growing dizziness?

Patience is wearing thin. You've been waiting ages for your turn in the shower, meticulously crafting the perfect shower playlist. But just as you inch closer, your siblings keep barging in, leaving you with nothing but cold, wet disappointment.

Feeling bold, you embark on a DIY hair dye adventure. You've meticulously followed the instructions, leaving the dye on for the recommended time. But a searing sensation erupts on your scalp – did you underestimate the dye's fiery power?

You're curling your hair and get distracted by your phone. You accidentally leave the hot curler on and burning a hole in the counter.

Sharing the bathroom with roommates means limited space for your toiletries. It seems like you never have enough room for your stuff.

You're hosting a party and a guest uses your favorite towel without asking.

You plug in your electric razor and notice several other appliances already using the outlet, including a hairdryer and a straightener. The outlet looks overloaded and the prongs are sparking slightly.

You reach for your bottle of body wash in the shower, but notice it feels lighter than usual. You pump it a few times, but nothing comes out. You peek over the shower curtain to see your sibling using your body wash!

You're in a rush to get out the door and quickly hop out of the shower without using a bath mat. Your foot lands on the wet tile floor, and you almost slip!

You're getting ready for a night out and the bathroom mirror is completely fogged up from the hot shower. Visibility is limited, making it difficult to see what you're doing while you are putting on eye makeup.

You open the bathroom door after a shower and are hit with a powerful wave of your brother's body spray. The smell is overwhelming and gives you a headache. You know some people have sensitivities to strong scents.

You're getting ready for school in the morning, but the bathroom is occupied by your siblings.

They're taking their time, and you're starting to get stressed about being late.

You step out of the shower, humming a happy tune, only to be met with a watery surprise. The shower curtain betrayed you, leaving a small ocean on the bathroom floor. Time to mop up this mess before someone takes a tumble!

A beady-eyed spider sits in the center of the bathtub, strategically positioned on the farthest point from the drain. Shrieks fill the air as you realize sharing the evening bath with this unwelcome guest is not part of the plan.

You're lathering up with your favorite shampoo, enjoying the steamy warmth, when suddenly the water flow falters and turns bone-chilling cold. A shiver runs down your spine as you realize a refreshing shower has become an arctic plunge.

Reaching for the toilet paper dispenser after a successful visit, your hand meets only emptiness. Panic starts to rise – how will you navigate this situation without your bathroom buddy?

You sprint through the school hallway, finally reaching the restroom. Relief washes over you – until you reach for the dispenser and find nothing but a sad, empty roll staring back. Act fast, gotta find a solution before nature calls again!

With a sigh of relief, you finish your business at the store restroom. But as you reach for the holy grail of bathroom essentials – disaster strikes. The dispenser taunts you with its

Jennifer Tillock M.S. CCC-SLP

emptiness. Will you brave asking an employee for help, or hold your breath and make a mad dash for the nearest exit?

You take your favorite new shampoo out of the shower and find most of it's gone! You suspect a sibling might have used it without asking.

You wince as your parent launches into a graphic description of their digestive woes through the bathroom door. Trying to create a spa-like shower experience is impossible with this embarrassing play-by-play as the soundtrack. Time to shut out the unwanted commentary!

You tap your foot impatiently, waiting for your turn in the shower. Your date is in thirty minutes, but your sibling seems to have transformed the bathroom into a personal concert hall. Their enthusiastic (but unfortunately off-key) singing is drowning out your attempts to focus on getting ready.

Stepping out of the shower, you're met with an obstacle course of your sibling's dirty clothes strewn across the bathroom floor. Socks, gym shorts, yesterday's t-shirt – it's like a laundry explosion! Navigating this gross obstacle course to get to your towel is not the post-shower pick-me-up you were hoping for.

Sharing the bathroom with siblings can be a challenge. You wait patiently for your turn in the shower, but the water keeps running and running.

You're rummaging through the medicine cabinet looking for some pain relievers, but everything seems unfamiliar. The labels are worn or outdated, and you're unsure what half the medications are for.

In a rush to get ready, you pump too much lotion onto your hands and it goes everywhere. The floor and counter are slick!

You're enjoying a relaxing bath when you hear the doorknob jiggle. You call out, "Occupied!" but the jiggling persists.

You're enjoying a relaxing shower, humming along to your favorite music, when the razor slips on your leg. A sharp sting jolts you back to reality – you've nicked yourself, and the blood starts to well up.

You're almost finished drying your hair after a refreshing shower when the unthinkable happens. The hair dryer suddenly sputters, sparks fly, and a burning smell fills the air.

You're adjusting the shower temperature, eager to find that perfect balance between hot and cold. Suddenly, the knob turns too far, and a blast of scalding water hits you. Pain shoots through your skin, and you instinctively jump back.

You reach for a fluffy towel after a relaxing shower, but the towel rack groans in protest. A precarious tower of damp towels teeters on the edge, threatening a full-on avalanche of terrycloth. Act fast, or bath time bliss turns into a laundry disaster.

You're humming along to your favorite song, lost in the post-shower glow, when the bathroom door bursts open. Startled and dripping wet, you face whoever dared interrupt your post-shower sanctuary.

You settle into the familiar privacy of the bathroom stall, ready to, well, use the facilities. But the sudden jiggling of the door handle sends a jolt of panic through you. Is someone trying to get in?

Reaching for your trusty minty toothpaste, you squeeze the tube with practiced ease. But wait, the expiration date screams back at you – months in the past! Do you risk a funky-flavored clean, or scramble to find a fresh tube?

You're getting ready in the morning and reach for your allergy meds. But the cabinet is dark and you accidentally grab the bottle next to it, which is your daily vitamin. Luckily, you realize your mistake before taking any.

You're getting ready in the morning and reach for your daily medication. The labels on two bottles look very similar.

You're in the middle of a relaxing bath when the lights suddenly flicker and go out. The bathroom is plunged into darkness, and you can't hear anything outside.

You fling open the bathroom door, ready to face the morning, but darkness greets you. The bathroom light bulb seems to have kicked the bucket – gotta get creative for your morning routine!

The bathroom counter is a battlefield of half-empty bottles and overflowing tubes. Finding your usual face wash feels like navigating a beauty product jungle – time to declutter!

Triumphantly, you hang your favorite fluffy towel on the bathroom door to dry after your shower. But later, returning for a warm hug of terrycloth, you find... nothing. The towel thief strikes again!

A pile of clothes lies nestled beside the bathroom heater, basking in its warmth. Perfect for a warm post-bath change, you think. But wait, using the heater means risking a wardrobe malfunction – a fashion disaster in the making!

Relief washes over you as you finish your shower. You reach for your trusty towel, ready to dry off, but your hand meets only empty air. Panic starts to set in – how will you face the world towel-less?

You lather up your hair with shampoo, enjoying the minty scent. Suddenly, the water flow sputters and dies. Confusion reigns – did the water bill get paid?

You crank up the bathroom heater for a toasty warm bath. But as the warmth spreads, a horrifying smell fills the air – burning hair! Did someone leave a rogue strand too close to the heat source?

You wear contact lenses and accidentally drop one in the sink while brushing your teeth. The water is running, and the contact is swirling down the drain!

Jennifer Tillock M.S. CCC-SLP

You leave your favorite towel hanging on the door to dry after your shower, but when you return, it's gone!

You're at a friend's house and see them vaping in the bathroom. You're uncomfortable with secondhand exposure and don't want to vape yourself.

Your bathroom gets really cold in the winter, so you like to put it close to the bathtub when you take a bath. You find it is best when you put it on the corner of the bathtub.

Strangers

Stranger Safety & Self-Advocacy for Teens: Be Street Smart & Speak Up!

The world is full of amazing people, but unfortunately, there are also those who might try to take advantage. Here are some tips to help you stay safe and feel empowered when interacting with strangers:

Stranger Danger:

- **Trust Your Gut:** If someone or a situation makes you feel uneasy, it probably is. Avoid the person or place and walk away confidently.

- **No is a Complete Sentence:** You are in control of your body and your time. Don't feel pressured to say yes to requests that make you uncomfortable. A simple, firm "no" is enough.

- **Buddy Up:** There's safety in numbers. Walk, bike, or hang out with a friend, especially in unfamiliar areas or after dark.

- **Let Someone Know:** Before you head out, especially if you're going somewhere new, tell a parent, guardian, or trusted adult where you're going and when you expect to be back.

- **Be Tech Savvy:** Keep your phone charged and location services enabled if possible. Consider sharing your location with a trusted adult through a tracking app (with their permission).

- **Know Your Surroundings:** Pay attention to your environment, not just your phone. Stay alert and avoid getting distracted by headphones or games when walking alone.

- **Stick to Public Places:** Avoid isolated areas, shortcuts through deserted parks, or poorly lit alleyways. Opt for well-lit and populated streets whenever possible.

- **Beware of Free Stuff:** Free puppies, rides, or "too-good-to-be-true" offers can be a lure. Stick with trusted adults and avoid situations that seem suspicious.

- **Don't Share Personal Info:** Don't give out your name, address, phone number, or school location to strangers. This includes online interactions as well.

- **If You Feel Unsafe:** Don't hesitate to yell for help, run to a safe place like a store or someone's house, or call 911 if necessary. Your safety is most important, and no one will be upset.

Self-Advocacy:

- **Know Your Rights:** You have the right to feel safe and respected by everyone.

- **Speak Up:** If someone is making you uncomfortable, don't be afraid to say something. Be direct and assertive. Make eye contact and use "I" statements to express your needs and concerns.

- **Set Boundaries:** It's okay to tell people "no" and to establish boundaries for how you want to be treated.

- **Don't Be Afraid to Ask Questions:** If you're unsure about something, don't be afraid to ask questions. It's better to clarify than to stay confused or uncomfortable.

- **It's Okay to Change Your Mind:** If you initially agree to something but later feel uncomfortable, it's okay to change your mind. Explain your situation and politely remove yourself from the situation.

- **Don't Be Afraid to Walk Away:** If a situation feels wrong, you have the right to walk away from it, even if it means missing out on something.

- **Trust Your Instincts:** If your gut tells you something isn't right, listen to it! Don't feel pressured to do something you're not comfortable with.

- **Talk to Someone You Trust:** If you've had a negative experience with a stranger, tell a parent, teacher, counselor, or another trusted adult.

Remember: If you ever feel unsafe, trust your gut and take action. Your safety and well-being are the most important things. Be confident, be aware, and don't hesitate to speak up for yourself!

- **National Teen Hotline:** 1-800-621-TEEN (8336)

- **Crisis Text Line:** Text HOME to 741741

- **Rape, Abuse & Incest National Network (RAINN):** 1-800-656-HOPE You can also get help online at RAINN: https://www.rainn.org

Jennifer Tillock M.S. CCC-SLP

Scenarios

You're leaving the library after dark and a knot of unease forms in your stomach. Glancing back, you see a man a few paces behind, seemingly lingering in the stacks as you move towards the exit. The streetlights cast long shadows, and the deserted sidewalk stretches before you.

You exit the store with your purchases, eager to reach your car. But a group of teenagers loitering by the doorway catches your eye. Their posture seems tense, and their gazes linger on you a beat too long as you approach the parking lot.

You're walking down the street, lost in thought, when you bump into someone carrying groceries. Their items scatter on the sidewalk, and you kneel down to help pick them up. The stranger seems overly grateful and insists on giving you a ride home as thanks. Despite their friendly demeanor, the situation feels strange.

You're at the park with friends when a stranger approaches, holding a lost dog. The dog appears malnourished and scared, and the stranger claims they found it wandering the streets. They ask if anyone recognizes the dog, but something about their story feels off.

You're at the gym, focused on your workout routine. A stranger approaches you mid-set, offering unsolicited advice on your form. Their attention feels intrusive, and their comments make you feel self-conscious.

Stepping off the bus, you head towards home. A nagging feeling makes you glance back and see someone who got off at the same stop walking in the same direction, maintaining a similar distance behind you. You adjust your grip on your backpack, the weight suddenly feeling more cumbersome.

You exit the late-night movie feeling tired, but a sense of unease prickles your skin as you reach the parking lot. Your car sits alone in a dimly lit corner, far from any other vehicles.

Relief washes over you as you reach the restroom after a long shopping trip. But as you step out, the door swings shut behind you, revealing another person entering the previously empty stall. Their presence feels wrong.

Leaving the store with your arms full of groceries, a man approaches, his voice laced with urgency. He explains his car is out of gas, and he desperately needs a ride to the nearest station. Despite his pleas, something about the situation makes you hesitate.

You enjoy your daily walk around the familiar neighborhood, but today a nagging feeling creeps in. A large truck seems to be circling the block, occasionally slowing down as it passes you.

Settling into your movie theater seat, you prepare to enjoy the film. However, the person next to you seems restless, their leg repeatedly bumping into yours. You politely shift in your seat, but the bumping continues.

While walking home alone after school, a stranger approaches, map clutched in hand. They explain they're lost and desperately need directions. Their kind smile seems genuine, but a flicker of unease sparks within you.

You're enjoying a walk in the park with your furry friend, their tail wagging happily. Suddenly, a stranger approaches, their gaze fixed on your dog. They launch into a flurry of compliments about your pet's looks, their body language seeming overly familiar. As they inch closer, your grip tightens on the leash, a flicker of unease sparking within you.

Lost in a labyrinth of clothes racks at the mall, you focus on picking out the perfect outfit. However, you can't shake the feeling of being watched. Glancing around, you spot a store employee following you closely, their eyes scanning your every move. Their excessive attention makes you feel increasingly uncomfortable.

Bored at home, you scroll through social media. A message pops up from an unknown profile, filled with compliments about your profile picture. Initially flattered, you respond politely. But the conversation takes a turn as the stranger starts asking for personal details, like your address and school.

You're waiting for your ride at a bus stop after dark. A group of teenagers huddles nearby, their loud laughter and boisterous behavior making you feel on edge. They keep glancing in your direction.

You're at a friend's house and their older sibling's friend offers to take you both home. While the friend seems nice, you don't know them well, and the idea of riding with a stranger makes you nervous.

You're walking home from a school dance alone. A car slows down beside you, and the driver, someone you recognize from a neighboring school, asks if you need a ride. You're tempted by the convenience.

The store doors shuts behind you with a heavy thud, the sound echoing in the empty parking lot. Evening shadows stretch long across the deserted sidewalk, and an unsettling feeling prickles your skin. Glancing back, you see a figure lingering in the doorway.

The party's energy is infectious, but a stranger's touch on your shoulder pulls you from the music. They introduce themselves, then ask for your social media handle. You barely know them, and their overly familiar grin makes you hesitate.

Lost in a new neighborhood, you fumble with your phone's map, frustration mounting. A friendly voice cuts through your worry – a stranger offering to walk you to your destination. Their smile seems genuine, but a flicker of doubt sparks within you.

Walking home from school, a car with tinted windows screeches to a halt beside you. The driver, a complete stranger, flashes a wad of cash and offers you a ride or a free gift. The opportunity is tempting, but something feels off about the situation.

Jennifer Tillock M.S. CCC-SLP

Lately, your new friend's texts have become increasingly demanding. They pressure you to hang out constantly and get upset if you don't answer right away. Their once playful messages morph into guilt trips and accusations. This shift in behavior makes you uncomfortable.

A group of teenagers catcall and follow closely behind you, their words laced with crude humor. Their unwanted attention makes you feel unsafe and harassed. Heart pounding, you consider your options to address the situation and escape their path.

Your friend beams with excitement, eager to set you up with someone they think you'd be perfect for. The problem? You've never met this person, and the idea of a blind date with an unknown stranger makes you nervous.

Panic sets in as you realize you've been separated from your friends in the crowded mall. A stranger approaches, offering help finding them.

Night falls as you wait for the bus. An unfamiliar person squeezes into the seat beside you, invading your personal space. Their close proximity makes you uneasy, and their persistent questions about your plans and whereabouts heighten your anxiety.

Leaving the theater after a late movie, a figure catches your eye in the rearview mirror. They seem to be following you down the deserted street, their pace mirroring yours. Fear grips you as you quicken your steps.

You stop a stranger for directions in a new neighborhood, but their instructions are confusing and seem to lead you further away from your destination. Lost and unsure, you question the validity of their information.

The library door swings shut with a heavy thud, the sound echoing in the deserted hallway. Evening shadows stretch long across the sidewalk, and an unsettling feeling prickles your skin. Glancing back, you see a figure in a hooded sweatshirt lingering by the doorway – are they following you?

The party's energy is infectious, but a stranger with a strong cologne scent taps your shoulder. They introduce themselves with a nickname and ask for your social media handle. Their eyes seem a little too bloodshot, and their overly familiar grin makes you hesitate.

You step into the elevator after a long day, eager to reach your floor. But you're the only one besides a stranger whose gaze darts nervously around. They keep muttering to themselves and pressing random buttons. An unsettling feeling creeps in.

You're enjoying a peaceful walk in the park, the sun warming your face. Suddenly, you spot a stranger peering intently into parked cars, their body language furtive. A prickle of unease runs down your spine.

Struggling to carry a heavy box filled with textbooks, you grunt with exertion. Just then, your kind neighbor from next door appears, offering help. Relief washes over you, but a nagging thought persists - is it safe to let

Jennifer Tillock M.S. CCC-SLP

someone you don't know well into your apartment?

The shortcut through the alley seems like a good idea until you round a corner and see a group of teenagers huddled together, their faces obscured by shadows. Their presence sends shivers down your spine.

Smoke billows from the hood of your car, stranded on a deserted stretch of road. Panic sets in, but then you see headlights in the distance. As the car gets closer, a lone driver emerges.

The party is loud, and the crowd feels overwhelming. You scan the room for your friends, but a sense of unease grows with every passing minute. The atmosphere feels strange, and you don't recognize many people.

Walking home alone after dark, you see a stranger pacing back and forth on the sidewalk ahead. They wave you down, their voice trembling as they ask for directions. Their body language seems tense, and a flicker of doubt sparks within you.

You're relaxing in the park with friends, enjoying a game of frisbee. Suddenly, a group of older kids approaches, their laughter loud and their stares lingering a little too long. They start circling your group and making suggestive comments, the situation escalating quickly.

Walking down the street, lost in your music, you bump into someone. They whirl around, their face contorted in anger. You apologize,

but they start yelling at you, their aggression making you feel threatened.

You're at a fast-food restaurant with your friends. While waiting in line, you notice a man following closely behind you, his gaze lingering a little too long on your backpack. He seems impatient and keeps muttering to himself. Unease prickles your skin.

You're browsing the aisles of a convenience store when a stranger approaches, asking for help finding a specific item. They seem genuinely lost, but their overly friendly demeanor makes you hesitate.

You're walking home after basketball practice, wearing your team jersey. A car with tinted windows slows down beside you, and the passengers start shouting taunts related to your team. Their aggressive behavior makes you feel threatened.

You're at the beach with a group of friends, enjoying a relaxing day in the sun. A group of older teenagers starts playing volleyball nearby, the ball repeatedly flying over the net and landing near you. Their laughter turns into jeering as they make inappropriate comments.

You're browsing clothes at a department store when a stranger strikes up a conversation about your outfit. They compliment your taste and offer to help you find other styles. While their attention feels flattering at first, it becomes excessive as they follow you around the store.

You're waiting for your ride outside a cafe, engrossed in a book. A stranger sits down next

Jennifer Tillock M.S. CCC-SLP

to you and starts asking intrusive questions about your plans for the evening. Their personal inquiries make you uncomfortable, and their body language seems overly familiar.

You're walking your dog in the park when you notice another dog owner approaching. As they get closer, their unleashed dog starts barking aggressively at your pet. Despite your attempts to calm the situation, the stranger seems unconcerned and makes no effort to restrain their animal.

You're at the mall with friends, trying on clothes in a fitting room. While you're changing, you hear someone enter the next stall. Moments later, you hear muffled sounds of someone taking pictures. Panic sets off alarm bells.

You're working on a school project at the library, using your laptop. A stranger wearing a long coat sits down at the computer next to you, but the position seems too close for comfort. Their body language makes you feel uneasy, and you suspect they might be trying to glance at your screen.

You're walking home from school with a classmate you don't know well. They start asking personal questions about your family life and living situation. Their excessive curiosity makes you uncomfortable, and you'd prefer to keep your personal details private.

You're helping your parents clean out the garage and come across an old phone in a box. Curious, you charge it up and discover it's still functional. However, upon opening it, you realize it's not your parents' phone and contains unfamiliar messages and photos.

You're leaving a school dance feeling tired but happy. As you wait for your ride, a group of older students you don't recognize approaches you. They start making suggestive comments and ask you to join their party. The situation feels unsafe, and their behavior makes you feel pressured. How do you politely decline their invitation and avoid escalating the situation?

Jennifer Tillock M.S. CCC-SLP

Home Alone Hero: A Comprehensive Guide to Safety and Self-Advocacy for Teens

Being a teenager often means navigating a world of newfound independence. Home alone time can be a chance to blast your favorite music, whip up a delicious snack, or simply relax in your own space. But with that freedom comes responsibility – the responsibility to ensure your safety and well-being in your own home. This guide is packed with tips and strategies to help you become a home alone hero, mastering both safety protocols and self-advocacy skills.

Safety First: Building a Fortress at Home

Our homes are sanctuaries, and ensuring their safety is paramount. Here's how to create a secure environment and be prepared for any situation:

- **Be an Emergency Expert:** Familiarize yourself with your home's emergency plan. Know the designated escape routes for fire or other emergencies. Practice the plan regularly with your family, including locating fire extinguishers and discussing meeting points outside the house.

- **Befriend the Fire Alarm:** Smoke detectors are lifesavers. Learn how to test them regularly (usually monthly) and replace batteries as needed. Replace the alarm itself every 10 years. Never disable the alarm, even for a burnt pizza!

- **Master the Mystery Box (First-Aid Kit):** Locate your family's first-aid kit and learn about its contents. Understand basic first-aid procedures for minor cuts, scrapes, or burns. If you're unsure, err on the side of caution and reach out to a trusted adult for help.

- **Weather the Storm:** Stay informed about weather forecasts. Download a weather app on your phone and keep an eye on potential storms or power outages. Have a plan in place for these situations, such as flashlights, battery-powered radios, and non-perishable snacks.

- **Be Wary of Unexpected Guests:** Don't open the door to strangers, even if they claim to be from a utility company or repair service you weren't expecting. Ask for identification and verify it with your parents before letting anyone in. Consider installing a peephole in your door for added security.

Safety Beyond the Basics: Proactive Measures for Everyday Life

Your home is more than just walls and a roof; it's full of potential hazards. Here's how to stay safe during everyday activities:

- **Kitchen Confidence:** The kitchen can be a dangerous place for the unprepared. When cooking alone, use caution with hot oil and sharp utensils. Always turn off appliances when you're finished and keep flammable materials like dish towels away from the stovetop.

- **Bathroom Blunders:** Slippery surfaces are a recipe for disaster. Take caution when stepping in and out of the shower or bath. Keep bath mats in place and avoid using electronic devices near water sources.

- **Electrical Engineering (Lite):** Damaged electrical cords or overloaded outlets pose a fire risk. Don't overload outlets and avoid using extension cords as a permanent solution. Unplug appliances when not in use and inform your parents if you notice any damaged electrical cords.

- **Chemical Caution:** Cleaning supplies and other household chemicals can be dangerous if not handled properly. Store them in a designated location out of reach of children and pets. Always read labels carefully and wear gloves when necessary.

- **Maintenance Matters:** Fix leaky faucets, replace flickering lightbulbs, and report any concerns about broken appliances to your parents promptly. Taking care of minor issues can prevent bigger problems in the future.

Self-Advocacy: Making Your Voice Heard

Being home alone isn't just about safety – it's about using your voice and making informed decisions. Here's how to advocate for yourself and your needs:

- **Be a Clear Communicator:** When discussing concerns about chores, house rules, or disagreements with family members, use clear and respectful language. Explain your perspective and back it up with reasons.

- **The Power of Knowledge:** If you believe a house rule is unfair, gather information to support your argument. For example, argue for a lighter chore load by highlighting the impact heavier chores have on your schoolwork or extracurricular activities.

- **The Art of Compromise:** Finding a solution that works for everyone is key. Be open to negotiation and propose alternatives that fulfill both your needs and your parents' expectations.

Jennifer Tillock M.S. CCC-SLP

- **Respect is a Two-Way Street:** While advocating for yourself, remember to respect your parents' perspectives and boundaries. Use a calm and assertive tone, avoiding accusatory language.

- **Speak Up for Safety:** Don't be afraid to voice concerns about safety issues, like expired food in the fridge or faulty appliances. Your well-being is paramount, and your voice matters.

Beyond Safety and Self-Advocacy: Building Confidence and Resourcefulness

Home alone time can be an opportunity for personal growth. Here are some ways to develop your skills and confidence while being home alone:

- **Become a Culinary Mastermind:** Use this time to experiment in the kitchen. Start with simple recipes and gradually build your skills. Not only will you be well-fed, but you'll also impress your family with your newfound culinary prowess when they return.

- **Channel Your Inner MacGyver:** Minor household problems can arise when you're home alone. A leaky faucet, a loose doorknob, or a clogged drain can seem daunting. However, with a little resourcefulness and a quick internet search, you might be surprised by how many simple fixes you can tackle yourself. Of course, for anything beyond your skillset, always consult a parent or trusted adult.

- **Embrace the Learning Opportunity:** Don't let home alone time become a screen-filled void. Use it to explore your interests. Read a book, work on a personal project, or tackle that online coding tutorial you've been eyeing.

- **Unleash Your Inner Artist:** Feeling creative? Home alone time is perfect for artistic endeavors. Draw, paint, write, or play an instrument - let your creative juices flow.

- **Connect with the World:** While independence is great, staying connected is important too. Call a friend, video chat with family, or join an online social group focused on your interests.

Bonus Tip: Prepare for the Unexpected – A Home Alone Survival Kit

Having a designated "home alone survival kit" can provide peace of mind and be helpful in unexpected situations. Here are some suggested items:

- Flashlight with extra batteries

- Battery-powered radio

- First-aid kit

- Non-perishable snacks and bottled water

- A list of important phone numbers (parents, emergency services, local trusted adult)

- A charged phone with a flashlight app - it's a good idea to have a backup battery for your phone (and keep it charged!)

- A small toolkit (screwdriver, pliers)

- A notebook and pen for keeping track of tasks or messages for your parents

Remember: Being home alone is a responsibility you can handle! Utilize the safety tips, self-advocacy strategies, and personal growth opportunities outlined here. By being prepared, informed, and confident, you can become a true home alone hero, navigating your independence with a sense of responsibility and personal empowerment.

Jennifer Tillock M.S. CCC-SLP

Scenarios

The blaring shriek of the tornado siren tears through the afternoon calm. A knot of dread forms in your stomach as you scan the darkening sky, unsure how quickly you need to seek shelter.

Your sister's forgotten hair clogs the shower drain, and your parents blame you for the mess. Frustration bubbles as you explain your innocence.

Alone at home, a sudden wheezing and tightness in your chest signal a serious allergic reaction. Grasping for your inhaler, you race to find it, battling the rising panic.

Walking to school, a nagging worry creeps in - did you remember to turn off the curling iron? Torn between the fear of a potential fire and the risk of being late, you contemplate your options.

Reaching for the doorknob, a wave of unease washes over you – the front door is ajar. No one else is supposed to be home. Heart pounding, you carefully peer inside to assess the situation.

You're helping your parents clean the attic and discover a box of old chemicals. Some containers are leaking, and you're unsure what the fumes might be.

The acrid screech of the smoke alarm fills the air. Instinct takes over as you remember your fire escape plan, scrambling towards the designated exit.

Home alone for the weekend, a sudden plunge in temperature coincides with the power cutting out. Bundling up in blankets, you huddle together for warmth, hoping for a speedy restoration.

A pungent odor of rotten eggs hangs heavy near the stove. Suspecting a gas leak, you immediately evacuate the house and call for help from a safe distance.

You are still getting the same amount of money for allowance that you were getting in second grade. You feel like you deserve more money since you are doing more chores.

Slamming the door shut, a horrifying realization dawns – your keys are still inside the house. Weighing your options, you contemplate calling a family member or finding a spare key hidden outside.

Reaching for the garbage bag, you're startled by a raccoon rummaging through the trash can. Backing away cautiously, you debate whether to scare it off or wait for it to finish its midnight snack.

You are ironing clothes for the family. A friend calls and you start talking and forget about the iron. When you come back, there is a hole burned in your dad's shirt and it is smoking.

You come home after school and find your younger sibling watching a movie that seems way too mature for them. You know you should say something, but you don't want to be a tattletale.

You're arguing with your parents about a curfew you think is unfair. You want to stay out later, but you don't want to disrespect them either.

You're stressed about an upcoming exam and can't seem to focus on studying. You consider taking a "study aid" someone at school mentioned, but you're worried about the potential consequences.

You're at home alone when a repair person arrives unexpectedly, claiming they were called to fix a problem you weren't aware of. They seem impatient and pushy, making you question their legitimacy.

You're enjoying a movie night with friends when the power suddenly cuts out. Visibility is limited, and you hear a faint sizzling sound coming from the kitchen. Uncertainty hangs in the air as you contemplate investigating the source or waiting for the power to return.

You're relaxing in your room when a strong gust of wind slams a window shut, shattering the glass. Shards litter the floor, and a cold draft cuts through the room. Fear and the urge to clean up battle with the knowledge you shouldn't touch broken glass.

You're taking a shower when the hot water suddenly cuts out, replaced by a concerning trickle of cold water. Confused and shivering, you debate whether to wait it out or investigate the cause of the sudden temperature change.

You're helping your parents unload groceries when you discover a carton of expired milk tucked away in the back of the fridge. Knowing it's unsafe to consume, you grapple with how to tell your parents without seeming picky.

You're home alone when a persistent knocking sound originates from the front door. Peeking through the peephole, you see a stranger holding a clipboard, claiming to be from a utility company you've never heard of. Uncertainty clouds your judgment as you decide whether to answer the door.

You're helping a family member with a project that requires physical labor you're uncomfortable with. You worry about hurting yourself but don't want to seem lazy or unhelpful.

You overhear your parents discussing a new family rule you strongly disagree with. Anxiety builds as you consider ways to voice your opinion without being disrespectful.

You're expected to attend a family gathering with relatives you find difficult. Stuck between wanting to spend time with loved ones and avoiding negative interactions, you wrestle with how to handle the situation.

You're assigned a chore you believe is unfair compared to the workload of your siblings. Feeling frustrated and unheard, you contemplate how to approach your parents and advocate for a more balanced distribution of responsibilities.

You're expected to participate in a family activity you find boring or embarrassing. Torn between wanting to please your family and expressing your individuality, you consider ways to communicate your feelings while still being a team player.

You're preheating the oven for dinner when the smoke alarm starts blaring. However, you see no smoke and the oven seems to be functioning normally. Confused, you debate whether to evacuate the house or investigate the source of the false alarm.

You're taking a relaxing bath when you notice a burning smell coming from the bathroom vent. Fear prickles your skin as you contemplate whether to investigate further or get help immediately.

You're cleaning your room and discover a strange, powdery substance on the floor. Unsure of its origin or potential dangers, you grapple with how to handle it safely.

You're leaving the house for school and notice a suspicious object left on the doorstep. Fear and curiosity battle within you as you decide whether to ignore it, alert a neighbor, or call the authorities.

You're helping your parents paint the house when you accidentally splatter paint on a valuable piece of furniture. Panic sets in as you weigh telling your parents immediately or trying to fix the mistake yourself.

You borrowed something from a sibling and accidentally broke it. Fear of their reaction battles with the knowledge you need to come clean and offer to replace it.

You're expected to wear a hand-me-down outfit to an important event, but you feel self-conscious about its style. Wrestling with wanting to fit in and expressing your personal style, you strategize a conversation with your parents about finding an alternative solution.

You're struggling with a school assignment and feel overwhelmed. Stuck between wanting to avoid trouble and advocating for yourself, you contemplate how to approach your teacher and ask for extra help.

You believe you deserve an allowance or increased responsibility, but your parents disagree. Determined to present your case, you gather evidence to support your request and prepare a convincing argument.

You wake up in the middle of the night to a loud banging noise coming from downstairs. Disoriented and scared, you debate whether to investigate the source of the sound or wake your parents.

You're enjoying a hot shower when the water pressure suddenly drops significantly. Concerned about a potential plumbing issue, you contemplate investigating further or waiting for the pressure to return to normal.

You're making a late-night snack in the kitchen when you notice a faint burning smell. Unable to identify the source, you weigh the risk of continuing to cook versus turning off the stove and investigating the odor.

You're relaxing in your room when a beeping sound starts coming from the smoke detector. However, you see no smoke and can't locate the source of the beeping. Uncertainty clouds your judgment as you decide whether to ignore it or treat it as a potential fire hazard.

You're helping your parents clean the garage and discover a container of unknown liquid with a faded label. Curious about its contents, you grapple with the knowledge that some household chemicals can be dangerous if not handled properly.

You're expected to babysit a younger sibling, but you have a prior commitment you made to a friend. Torn between family responsibility and honoring your word to a friend, you strategize how to communicate the situation to both parties.

You believe you're being blamed for something you didn't do. Frustration and anger simmer as you consider the best way to defend yourself and clear your name.

You're struggling with a part-time job and feel overwhelmed by the workload. Torn between wanting to keep your job and advocating for yourself, you contemplate how to approach your employer and discuss a more manageable schedule.

You're enjoying a movie marathon with friends when a sudden power outage plunges the house into darkness. Candles are lit, but flickering shadows and unfamiliar noises from outside raise concerns. You must decide how to stay safe and maintain a sense of calm until the power returns.

A heavy downpour batters the house, and you hear a concerning crack from the attic. Worried about a potential roof leak or structural damage, you must determine how to investigate safely without putting yourself at risk.

You discover a strange insect infestation in your room. Concerned about potential bites or property damage, you must identify the insects and determine the safest way to remove them from your living space.

You're replacing a lightbulb in a high ceiling fixture when the stepladder wobbles precariously. Frightened and stuck mid-air, you must figure out how to climb down safely or call for help without risking a fall.

You disagree with a new house rule your parents have implemented. Feeling unheard and frustrated, you must find a respectful way to voice your concerns and propose a compromise solution.

You're expected to participate in a family tradition you find outdated or uncomfortable. Torn between respecting your family's customs and expressing your individuality, you must navigate the situation in a way that honors both perspectives.

You believe you're being pressured to take on more chores than your siblings. Feeling resentful and overworked, you must learn to advocate for a more balanced distribution of household responsibilities within the family.

Jennifer Tillock M.S. CCC-SLP

Around Town/Outdoors

Navigating the World: Safety and Self-Advocacy for Teens

The world is a vast and exciting place, but venturing out requires both **safety awareness** and the ability to **advocate for yourself**. This guide combines essential tips to empower you to have enriching and safe experiences around town and outside.

General Safety Principles

- **Planning is Power:** Research your destination before you go. Understand traffic patterns, opening hours, and potential weather conditions. Inform a trusted adult about your whereabouts and estimated return time. Planning your route is crucial, especially on unfamiliar trails.
- **Buddy Up:** There's safety in numbers. Explore with friends whenever possible. Having someone by your side can deter unwanted attention and provide assistance in case of emergencies. For solitary activities, inform someone about your route and estimated return time.
- **Charge Up:** Your phone is a lifeline. Ensure it's fully charged before heading out. Consider carrying a portable charger for extended outings.
- **Be Visible:** Wear bright clothing during the day, especially if you're biking or running. Invest in reflective gear for nighttime activities.
- **Listen Up:** Minimize headphone use, especially on busy streets or unfamiliar trails. Staying aware of your surroundings through sound is essential for safety.
- **Know Your Limits:** Pace yourself. Don't overexert on hikes or bike rides, especially in hot weather. Listen to your body and take breaks when needed. Dehydration can be serious, so carry a water bottle and replenish fluids regularly.
- **Beware of Strangers:** While most people are friendly, it's important to remain cautious. Don't share personal information with strangers. Avoid isolated areas, especially at night.
- **Trust Your Gut:** If you feel uncomfortable in a situation, remove yourself immediately. It's okay to say "no" and walk away.

Additional Considerations

- **Self-Defense Awareness:** While avoiding confrontation is always best, it's helpful to be aware of basic self-defense techniques. Consider taking a self-defense class to feel more confident and prepared.
- **Cyber Safety:** The online world can be just as dangerous as the physical one. Be mindful of what you share online and avoid meeting strangers you met online in person.
- **Financial Safety:** Only carry the essential amount of cash when exploring. Use secure payment methods and be cautious about using ATMs in isolated areas.
- **Personal Belongings:** Keep your belongings secure, especially valuables like your phone and wallet. Avoid carrying anything you wouldn't mind losing. Consider investing in a small backpack or purse that allows for hands-free movement

Safety by Location: Specific Tips for Different Environments

This section will delve deeper into specific safety and self-advocacy strategies for various locations:

On the Streets:

- **Pedestrian Power:** Follow traffic signals meticulously. Look both ways before crossing the street, even at crosswalks. Avoid distractions like texting while walking. Stay alert to cyclists and motorized vehicles.
- **Jaywalking is Risky:** Crossing outside designated crosswalks is dangerous. Wait patiently for the light to turn green, even if it feels slow.
- **Be Assertive on Sidewalks:** If a group of people are walking several abreast, impeding your path, politely excuse yourself and ask for some space to pass.

Public Transportation:

- **Stay Alert:** Be aware of your surroundings while waiting for buses or trains. Stand in well-lit areas and avoid isolated bus stops at night. Keep valuables secure and avoid displaying them openly.
- **Know Your Exit:** Familiarize yourself with emergency exits on buses and trains before you ride.
- **Report Unwanted Attention:** If someone makes you feel uncomfortable with inappropriate comments or advances, don't hesitate to inform the bus driver or a security guard.

Parks and Trails:

- **Plan Your Route:** Choose well-maintained, well-traveled trails, especially for solo adventures. Inform someone about your intended route and estimated return time.
- **Weather Woes:** Check the weather forecast before heading out. Be prepared for sudden changes. Pack rain gear if necessary and avoid venturing out during storms.

Jennifer Tillock M.S. CCC-SLP

- **Wildlife Encounters:** Wildlife encounters can be exciting, but maintain a safe distance. Never attempt to feed or approach wild animals.
- **Leave No Trace:** Respect the environment. Pack out all your trash and avoid disturbing natural habitats.
- **Respectful Enjoyment:** If a group is taking up excessive space on a trail, hindering your progress, politely ask them to give you some room to pass.

Service Establishments:

- **Food Safety:** When ordering food, inform the waiter/waitress about any allergies you have. Be cautious if you suspect food poisoning. If you experience stomach upset after eating, contact the restaurant and potentially seek medical advice.
- **Beware of Overcharging:** Double-check your bill for any discrepancies. Politely address any mistakes with a staff member.
- **Lost and Found:** If you lose your belongings in a store, inform a staff member immediately and describe the lost item in detail.

Entertainment Venues:

- **Fire Safety:** When entering a cinema or theatre, locate fire exits and familiarize yourself with evacuation procedures.
- **Volume Control:** Loud noises, especially in concerts or movies, can damage your hearing. Consider using earplugs if necessary.
- **Seating Etiquette:** Recline your seat in a movie theater only as much as it doesn't obstruct the view of the person behind you. Be mindful of others in your surroundings and avoid disruptive behavior.

Taxis and Ubers:

- **Verify Information:** Before entering any taxi or Uber, confirm the license plate matches the information in your app. Double-check the driver's photo and name to ensure they align with your booking details. If anything seems off, wait for a different ride.
- **Trust Your Gut:** If you feel unsafe at any point during the ride, don't hesitate to speak up. You can politely ask the driver to pull over in a well-lit, public area or request to be dropped off at the nearest safe location.
- **Communication is Key:** Don't be afraid to communicate your needs to the driver. If you're uncomfortable with the temperature, music, or route, politely ask them to adjust accordingly. Feeling unwell due to strong odors or a lack of seatbelt use by the driver? Voice your concerns and request a change.
- **Plan Ahead:** Keep your phone charged whenever possible. This allows you to track your ride using the app, contact someone in case of an emergency, or use a ride-sharing safety feature like sharing your live location.
- **Know Your Options:** Familiarize yourself with the terms and conditions of the ride-sharing service you're using. Knowing your payment options, cancellation policies, and reporting procedures empowers you to handle unexpected situations.

Emergency Situations

- **Know the Emergency Numbers:** Memorize emergency contact numbers for your area, including police, ambulance, and fire department.
- **Stay Calm:** In an emergency, remain composed. Panicking can cloud your judgment. Assess the situation and prioritize your safety. If you're with friends, delegate tasks and work together.
- **Seek Help:** If injured, call for help immediately. Utilize your phone to dial emergency services or flag down a passerby for assistance.
- **First Aid Knowledge:** Having basic first aid knowledge can be invaluable in an emergency. Learn how to perform CPR and treat minor injuries like cuts and sprains.
- **Report Suspicious Activity:** If you witness a crime or suspicious activity, report it to a trusted adult or directly to the authorities.

Finding Your Voice: Self-Advocacy Tips for Teens

Building Confidence

- **Know Yourself:** The foundation of self-advocacy is self-awareness. Understand your strengths, weaknesses, and boundaries. What makes you feel comfortable or uncomfortable? What situations might require you to speak up for yourself?
- **Practice Makes Perfect:** Self-advocacy doesn't always come naturally. Practice expressing your needs and opinions in low-pressure situations. Talk to friends, family, or trusted adults about how you feel or what you need.

Communicate Clearly

- **Be Direct:** When advocating for yourself, speak in a clear, concise, and respectful manner. State your needs or concerns directly, avoiding phrases like "I think" or "maybe" which can weaken your message.
- **Body Language Matters:** Maintain good posture, make eye contact, and use a confident tone of voice. Nonverbal communication can significantly impact how your message is received.
- **Active Listening:** Pay attention to the other person's response. Listen actively, clarify any misunderstandings, and be prepared to adjust your approach if needed.

Jennifer Tillock M.S. CCC-SLP

Self-Advocacy by Location: Tips Tailored to Different Environments

Knowing how to speak up for yourself is an important part of staying safe. Here are some tips on how to use your self-advocacy skills in different situations:

On the Streets:

- **Feeling Uncomfortable:** If someone is following you too closely or making inappropriate comments, **speak up clearly and directly**. Tell them to leave you alone and walk in the opposite direction.
- **Needing Assistance:** If you're lost or need help crossing a busy street, **don't be afraid to ask a trusted adult, police officer, or store employee** for assistance.
- **Witnessing a Crime:** If you see a crime being committed, **report it to a trusted adult or call the police**. Don't be afraid to intervene if you can do so safely.

Public Transportation:

- **Uncomfortable with a Passenger:** If someone on the bus or train is making you feel uncomfortable with loud music, offensive language, or unwanted advances, **politely but firmly ask them to stop**. If they don't, inform the bus driver or a security guard.
- **Inaccurate Fare:** If the bus driver asks you to pay a fare you think is incorrect, **politely ask them to explain the charge**. You can also request a receipt for your records.
- **Feeling Unsafe Getting Off:** If you feel unsafe getting off at your stop, especially at night, **ask the driver if they can drop you off at a better-lit location**.

Parks and Trails:

- **Encountering Aggressive Animals:** If you encounter an aggressive animal, **don't run**. Maintain eye contact and slowly back away. Report the encounter to a park ranger or another adult.
- **Disrespectful Trail Users:** If a group of people are blocking the trail and ignoring your attempts to pass politely, **don't be afraid to speak up more firmly**. Let them know you'd like to pass and ask them to move to the side.
- **Lost or Injured:** If you get lost or injured on a trail, **use your phone to call for help**. If you don't have cell service, try to find a ranger station or another person for assistance.

Service Establishments:

- **Food Allergies:** Don't be shy about asking questions about ingredients when ordering food. **Clearly communicate any allergies you have** and inquire about potential allergens in dishes.
- **Dissatisfied with Service:** If you receive poor service at a restaurant or shop, **calmly explain the situation to a manager**. Politely request a solution, such as a replacement meal or a refund.

- **Overcharged Bill:** If you notice an error on your bill at a restaurant or store, **point it out to the cashier or waiter/waitress** in a polite manner. Explain the discrepancy and request a corrected bill.

Entertainment Venues:

- **Disruptive Behavior:** If someone's behavior in a movie theater or concert is ruining your experience, **politely ask them to stop**. If the behavior persists, inform a staff member and request their intervention.
- **Uncomfortable Seating:** If the person in front of you at a movie theater reclines their seat excessively, blocking your view, **politely ask them to adjust it slightly**.
- **Lost Belongings:** If you lose your belongings at a venue, **immediately report it to a staff member**. Describe the lost item in detail and ask if they have a lost and found.

Taxis and Ubers:

- **Route Concerns:** If the driver takes a route you're unfamiliar with or uncomfortable with, **ask them to explain why**. You can also use the app to track the route and compare it to the expected path.
- **Unsafe Driver:** If you feel unsafe because of the driver's behavior, speeding, or lack of seatbelt use, **speak up immediately**. Ask them to pull over in a safe location and let you out. If necessary, call the police or a trusted adult for help.
- **Unclear Charges:** If the final fare displayed on the app is significantly higher than what you expected, **politely ask the driver to explain the charges**. Refer to the ride-sharing service's terms and conditions if needed.

Remember, self-advocacy is about feeling empowered to speak up for your safety and well-being. By using your voice effectively, you can navigate your surroundings with more confidence and control.

Additional Resources

- **Self-Advocacy Workshops:** Consider attending workshops or seminars designed to teach self-advocacy skills specifically for teens.
- **Online Resources:** Look for online resources and articles that provide tips and strategies for effective communication and self-advocacy.

Remember: Self-advocacy is a powerful tool that empowers you to navigate the world around you with confidence and control. Here are some additional points to remember:

- **Be Assertive, Not Aggressive:** There's a difference between being assertive and aggressive. Assertiveness involves clearly communicating your needs while respecting the rights of others. Avoid yelling, using accusatory language, or resorting to personal attacks.

Jennifer Tillock M.S. CCC-SLP

- **De-escalate When Possible:** If a situation becomes confrontational, try to de-escalate by remaining calm and respectful. If the situation worsens, remove yourself from the situation and seek help from a trusted adult or authority figure.
- **Know When to Walk Away:** Sometimes, the best course of action is to walk away from a situation that makes you feel uncomfortable or unsafe. Don't be afraid to remove yourself from a conversation or activity that doesn't align with your values or boundaries.
- **Practice Makes Progress:** Self-advocacy is a skill that takes time and practice to develop. Don't get discouraged if you don't always get the outcome you desire. The more you practice communicating your needs, the more comfortable and confident you'll become.
- **The Power of "No":** Learning to say "no" is a crucial aspect of self-advocacy. Don't feel pressured to participate in activities or conversations that make you feel uncomfortable. A polite but firm "no" is a complete sentence.

Self-Advocacy and the Law

As a teenager, you have certain legal rights that can empower you to advocate for yourself in specific situations. These rights may vary depending on your location, but here are some general examples:

- **Right to Refuse Service:** Businesses cannot discriminate against you based on factors like race, religion, or gender identity. You have the right to refuse service if you feel a business is treating you unfairly.
- **Right to Privacy:** You have a right to privacy regarding your personal information. Be cautious about sharing personal details with strangers, and understand your rights regarding data collection practices.
- **Right to Fair Treatment:** You have the right to be treated fairly in public places. If you witness or experience discrimination, you have the right to report the incident to the appropriate authorities.

The Importance of Bystander Intervention

Self-advocacy extends beyond just speaking up for yourself. It's also about advocating for others who may be unable to speak up for themselves. If you witness someone being harassed or treated unfairly, consider intervening in a safe and respectful manner. Here are some tips for safe bystander intervention:

- **Distraction:** Try to distract the person being harassed by starting a conversation or asking a question.
- **Direct Intervention:** If the situation allows, politely but firmly ask the person harassing the other person to stop.
- **Seek Help:** If you feel unsafe intervening directly, find a trusted adult or authority figure and report the incident.

Conclusion

Developing strong self-advocacy skills empowers you to navigate the world with confidence and control. By learning to communicate your needs effectively, assert your boundaries, and stand up for yourself and others, you'll be well-equipped to face challenges and create positive experiences in your surroundings. Remember, you have the right to speak up for your safety and well-being.

Jennifer Tillock M.S. CCC-SLP

Scenarios

Panic starts to set in as you pat your pockets (or rummage through your bag). Your wallet/purse containing your ID, credit cards, and cash seems to have vanished. Was it left at the coffee shop, or did it fall out on the bus?

You have a severe peanut allergy, and although you informed the waiter of your allergy when ordering, a stray peanut is present in your dish. You begin to feel the tell-tale signs of an allergic reaction.

You're texting a friend, engrossed in a conversation, as you walk along a busy sidewalk. Suddenly, a jogger appears from around a corner, heading straight for you. Caught off guard, you have mere seconds to react and avoid a collision.

Running late to meet up with friends, you see a clear break in traffic across a busy intersection. Ignoring the red pedestrian light, you decide to jaywalk to save time. Halfway across, a car speeds through the yellow light, forcing you to scramble out of the way.

The bus screeches to a halt, throwing you off balance. You reach for a handhold as a crowd of passengers surges forward to get off. In this jostle, you feel someone brush against your backpack. Glancing back, you see a glimpse of a hand reaching for your pocket.

You're browsing the shelves in a clothing store, a stack of shirts balanced precariously in your arms. Suddenly, a display topples over, sending hangers and clothes scattering across the floor. Caught off guard, you stumble and one of the shirts falls, landing in a puddle of spilled soda. Now you're faced with a damaged item and a potential mess.

Lost in the maze of aisles in a large hardware store, you reach for a heavy toolbox on a high shelf. As you pull, the box feels heavier than expected and starts to tilt forward. Panicked, you struggle to hold it back.

You're waiting for your Uber outside a restaurant late at night. The car you ordered looks different from the picture in the app, and the driver doesn't seem to know your name. Do you get in the car, or do you wait for a different one?

You hail a taxi on a busy street, but when you get in, you notice the driver isn't wearing a seatbelt. You feel uncomfortable, but you're not sure if it's appropriate to say something. What do you do?

You're taking a taxi home after a party with friends. The driver seems lost and keeps taking unfamiliar back roads. You start to feel nervous and wonder if you should ask them to use GPS navigation. How can you politely address the situation?

You're hanging out with your friends at the park, tossing a frisbee back and forth as music pumps from a portable speaker. You catch the frisbee mid-air, feeling the cool plastic against your fingertips, and prepare to throw it back when a loud crack echoes across the field. You squint towards the bright flash of lightning that comes a second later.

You book an Uber to go to the mall, but when you get in, the car smells strongly of cigarette smoke. You have asthma and the smoke is making it difficult to breathe. Do you stay silent and hope for the short ride to be over, or do you politely ask the driver to open a window or pull over for some fresh air?

The traffic is heavy, and your taxi ride is taking much longer than expected. You're worried you might be late for your curfew, and you're also conscious of the increasing fare cost. What can you do to manage the situation?

You're sharing a cab with a stranger who seems intoxicated and keeps making inappropriate comments. You feel unsafe and want the ride to end as soon as possible. How can you communicate your discomfort to the driver and potentially get out at a safe location earlier?

Your phone is about to die, and you need to use the Uber app to track your ride home and stay connected. You don't have a portable charger, and you're worried about being stranded without a way to contact anyone. What can you do to ensure you have a safe ride home?

You're getting into a taxi after a movie, and you realize you forgot your wallet at home. You only have your phone with you, and you're not sure if the driver accepts cashless payments. How can you address this situation without getting stranded?

You hail a taxi during a downpour, and you notice the windshield wipers aren't working properly. Visibility seems limited, and you're concerned about the driver's ability to see clearly. What can you do to prioritize your safety in this situation?

You book an Uber to go to a friend's house in an unfamiliar neighborhood. As you near your destination, you realize you might not have the exact address memorized. How can you communicate your location effectively with the driver to ensure a smooth drop-off?

You're trying on a new pair of shoes in a crowded store. The fitting room is tiny, and you accidentally knock over a display of sunglasses with your elbow. The sound of shattering glass fills the air.

Standing in line at the checkout, you witness a cashier arguing with another customer about a price discrepancy. The situation escalates, and the cashier becomes visibly flustered. You feel uncomfortable with the growing tension.

Reaching for a box of cereal on a high shelf at the grocery store, you lose your balance and wobble precariously. You grab for the shelf to steady yourself, but a can of soup tumbles off and crashes to the floor, splattering the contents everywhere. You are embarrassed and worried about the mess.

Trying on a new swimsuit in a fitting room, you realize the clasp on the back is broken and you can't get it undone. Stuck in the swimsuit, you feel frustrated and a little embarrassed.

Jennifer Tillock M.S. CCC-SLP

The weight room is bustling with activity. You approach a machine you've never used before, eager to try a new exercise. However, the instructions are unclear and there are no diagrams. Lifting weights without proper form can lead to injury.

You're lifting weights with a friend, spotting each other for safety. Your friend attempts a heavier weight than usual and struggles to complete the set. You are concerned about their form and potential injury

Midway through your workout, you feel a sharp pain in your knee. Ignoring minor aches is normal, but this pain feels different and persistent. Continuing to exercise could worsen the injury.

You're browsing the electronics section, completely engrossed in the latest phone model. Lost in the world of tech specs, you bump into another shopper, sending their phone tumbling to the ground. The screen cracks on impact.

Standing in line to pay for your purchases, you notice the cashier accidentally scans the same item twice on your receipt. The total is significantly higher than expected, but the cashier seems oblivious.

You're flipping through a magazine in the waiting area of the hair salon, excited about your new haircut. However, as you glance at the stylist cutting someone else's hair, you notice they're using rusty or dull scissors. You're feeling a little worried about the safety of the scissors.

Midway through your manicure, you notice the nail technician accidentally nicks your cuticle with the clippers. A small bead of blood wells up, and you feel a sharp sting. You are concerned about hygiene and potential infection.

You're getting your ears pierced for the first time. The piercer explains the aftercare instructions, but you're feeling nervous and overwhelmed with the information overload.

You're getting your eyebrows waxed for the first time. The technician applies the hot wax, but it feels much hotter than you anticipated. You are worried about getting burned.

While getting a spray tan, the technician asks you to raise your arms in an awkward position. You start to feel dizzy and lightheaded, and your legs begin to wobble.

You're at the gym for a weightlifting session. You're about to attempt a new exercise on a machine you're unfamiliar with. However, the instructions are unclear, and there's no staff member readily available.

Sitting in the massage chair, the masseuse applies a deep tissue massage. While some pressure is expected, the intensity becomes increasingly painful.

You're walking through the store with your friends, chatting and laughing. One of your friends picks up a hat and jokingly puts it on without paying. A security guard approaches, eyeing them suspiciously. You feel caught in an awkward situation – how will you de-escalate the situation and assure the guard your friend has no intention of stealing?

Reaching for a jar of jam on a high shelf, you misjudge the distance and knock it over. The jar shatters on the floor, sending glass shards flying and sticky jam everywhere.

The bus driver announces a sudden detour due to a road closure. You're unfamiliar with the new route, and your stop isn't listed among the upcoming announcements.

The bus groans to a halt, the air thick with smoke. A burnt rubber smell fills your nostrils, and panicked murmurs ripple through the passengers. You cough, realizing there might be a fire on board.

Visiting a new part of town, you're relying on your phone map to navigate. Focused on the screen, you don't notice the uneven sidewalk until you trip and fall, scraping your knee on the rough pavement. Feeling shaken and lost, you need to figure out how to continue your journey safely.

You're relaxing by the pool with friends, enjoying the sunshine. Lost in conversation, you don't realize how much time has passed. Suddenly, you feel a sunburn starting to develop on your shoulders.

You're about to jump into the pool for a refreshing dip. However, you notice a group of teenagers playing a boisterous game of Marco Polo, making it difficult to see clearly underwater. Concerned about potential collisions, how will you navigate this situation and ensure you can enter the pool safely?

You're splashing around in the shallow end when you accidentally step on a broken flip flop left at the bottom of the pool. The sharp plastic cuts your foot, and blood starts welling up. In pain and concerned about infection, how will you alert a lifeguard and get help treating the wound?

You're swimming laps when you experience a muscle cramp in your leg. Panicked and unable to move freely, you start to struggle and sink underwater. Unable to call for help verbally, how will you signal to a lifeguard that you're in distress and need assistance?

You're at the pool with a younger sibling who's still learning to swim. They excitedly run towards the deep end, unaware of the danger. Realizing the potential for trouble, how will you calmly but firmly intervene and ensure your sibling stays safe in the shallow water?

You're relaxing by the pool when you notice a group of teenagers running around the pool deck, shoving each other playfully. One of them slips and falls headfirst into the shallow end, landing with a thud. Concerned about a potential head injury, how will you assess the situation and determine if a lifeguard needs to be called?

You're about to enter the pool when you see a cloudy film on the water's surface and a strong chlorine smell. The pool might not be properly maintained, which could irritate your eyes and skin.

You're enjoying a swim when you notice a storm brewing in the distance. Dark clouds roll in, and the wind picks up. Lightning flashes illuminate the sky.

You're at a crowded public pool with limited shade options. You spend most of the time in direct sunlight, and you're starting to feel dizzy and nauseous. These might be symptoms of heatstroke.

You're swimming with friends when you see a child alone and crying at the edge of the pool. They don't seem to know how to swim and might be in danger.

Walking home alone after dark, you notice a group of older teenagers following you. Their whistles and catcalls make you feel uncomfortable and unsafe.

Approaching a busy intersection, you realize the traffic light is malfunctioning and completely dark. Cars are whizzing through the intersection in a chaotic dance. Unsure of who has the right of way, you hesitate, unsure how to cross the street safely.

You glance at your restaurant bill and notice you've been charged for an item you didn't order. Feeling unsure and a bit embarrassed, how will you politely bring this mistake to the waiter's attention?

You're enjoying a meal with friends when a group at a nearby table starts making inappropriate comments and gestures towards you. You feel harrassed and uncomfortable.

You're at a friend's party, enjoying the music and socializing. However, the house is packed with people, and the temperature is starting to feel stifling. The air feels thick and humid, and you're starting to sweat. You're worried about overheating.

You're at a party with a large group you don't know well. The conversation lulls, and you feel a bit awkward standing alone. You want to connect with others, but are unsure how to break into established groups

You're at a party where some teenagers are playing a drinking game. You're uncomfortable with alcohol and don't want to participate.

You're at a party where the music is extremely loud. You're enjoying the party atmosphere, but the volume is starting to cause discomfort in your ears. You're worried about possible hearing damage.

You're at a party where someone spills a drink on your favorite outfit. The stain is noticeable, and you feel frustrated. You are annoyed but unsure how to react.

You're at a party where someone offers you an unfamiliar substance. Unsure what it is and concerned about the potential risks, how will you politely refuse the offer and explain you're not interested?

You're at a party where a group of teenagers is vaping in a corner. The secondhand smoke irritates your throat and eyes.

You're at a party where the host announces a game that involves messy dares. You're not interested in getting messy and would prefer to watch.

The previews are rolling, and you're excited to settle in for the movie. However, the group in front of you reclines their seats all the way back, blocking most of your view of the screen.

You're enjoying the movie when a loud group of teenagers arrives and starts talking loudly and laughing throughout the previews. Their disruptive behavior is distracting and ruins the experience for others.

You reach for your popcorn during a particularly intense scene in the movie, only to discover the entire bag is empty. You're hungry and disappointed, but the movie is already halfway through.

The movie trailer before your feature film advertises a horror flick filled with jump scares. You're not a huge fan of horror movies and know you'll likely get scared. However, your friends are excited to see it.

You settle into your seat, ready for the movie, but a strong smell of perfume wafts up from the person sitting next to you. The scent is overwhelming and gives you a headache.

The movie is dark and suspenseful, and the sound effects are booming. Suddenly, you experience a sharp pain in your ear, and your hearing feels muffled. You are concerned about a potential earache or hearing damage.

You bought your movie ticket online and reserved your seat in advance. However, when you arrive, you discover someone is already sitting in your assigned seat.

You're halfway through the movie when you spill your drink all over yourself. Embarrassed and sticky, you feel uncomfortable staying in your seat. How will you decide whether to discreetly leave the theater to clean up and risk missing part of the movie?

The previews are rolling, and you realize you forgot to turn your phone on silent. Suddenly, your phone rings loudly, disrupting the quiet theater.

The movie is nearing its climax, and the tension is high. Suddenly, you feel a wave of nausea come over you. You are concerned you might get sick.

The party host announces there will be a bonfire later in the evening. You're excited about the idea, but you have asthma and smoke can trigger your condition.

You're at a party and suddenly feel a wave of nausea come over you. You realize you might be getting sick. You are concerned about spreading germs and want to avoid further discomfort.

A few hours after eating at the restaurant, you start experiencing stomach cramps and nausea. Suspecting food poisoning, you need to decide whether to stay home and rest or reach out to the restaurant to report the incident.

You're at a restaurant with a large group of friends, and someone suggests splitting the bill evenly, including the tip. However, the service was slow and inattentive.

You're cruising along on your bike, lost in the latest episode of your favorite podcast playing through your headphones. Suddenly, a car door swings open in front of you, leaving you with hardly any time to react.

Jennifer Tillock M.S. CCC-SLP

You approach a busy intersection with multiple lanes of traffic. Cars are whizzing by, and the light seems to take forever to turn green. Feeling pressured by traffic behind you, you contemplate running the red light to avoid holding up cars.

You're enjoying a scenic bike ride on a remote trail when your tire goes flat. Without a spare tube or pump, you're stranded miles from home.

You're hiking a new trail with friends, excited to explore the scenery. However, the trail gets progressively steeper and rockier than you anticipated. You're not comfortable with the challenging terrain and worried about slipping or injuring yourself. How will you communicate your concerns to your friends and suggest a less difficult route back?

You're enjoying a bike ride on a sunny day, but haven't packed enough water. As you continue your ride, you start to feel thirsty and a bit lightheaded. Dehydration can be serious, especially in hot weather. How will you prioritize your safety, decide when to turn back, and find a way to rehydrate?

You're walking your dog in the park when you encounter another dog off leash. Your dog is leash-trained but tends to be reactive around unfamiliar animals. Concerned about a potential fight, how will you politely communicate with the other dog owner and ensure a safe encounter for both animals?

You're having a picnic lunch in the park when a swarm of bees descends on your food. You're allergic to bee stings, and the situation makes you nervous. How will you calmly gather your belongings, keep a safe distance from the bees, and find a new location to enjoy your lunch?

You're exploring a new park with friends when you stumble upon a group of teenagers skateboarding on a designated walking path. Their reckless behavior creates a safety hazard for pedestrians. How will you politely address the situation and ask them to find a safer location for their skateboarding activity?

You're enjoying a frisbee game with friends in the park when the frisbee gets stuck high up in a tree branch. Climbing the tree to retrieve it could be dangerous. How will you decide whether to leave the frisbee behind and continue your game, or try to find a safe way to get it down?

You're hiking on a familiar trail when you notice dark clouds gathering in the distance. The weather can change quickly, and a sudden downpour could be dangerous on the trail. How will you assess the weather conditions and decide whether to continue your hike or seek shelter until the storm passes?

You're walking your dog in the park when you notice a broken glass bottle on the ground. Broken glass can be a hazard for both humans and animals. How will you safely dispose of the glass bottle to prevent injuries and ensure the safety of others using the park?

You're jogging on a secluded trail when you twist your ankle on an uneven patch of ground. The pain is sharp, and you're unable to put any weight on your ankle. Being alone and potentially injured requires action. How will you assess the situation and determine if you can walk back for help or need to call for assistance?

The sun is setting fast, casting long shadows across the bike path. You realize your bike doesn't have a headlight or taillight, making you nearly invisible to oncoming traffic.

You're out for a fun bike ride with a group of friends. One of your friends, known for being a bit of a daredevil, attempts a risky maneuver and ends up swerving into oncoming traffic.

You head out for a bike ride with a light jacket, expecting clear skies. Suddenly, dark clouds roll in and a downpour begins. Soaked and miles from home, you need to find shelter and a way to stay safe until the storm passes.

The stylist steps back with a flourish, revealing your new haircut. But something isn't right. One side seems noticeably shorter than the other.

You take a triumphant bite of your perfectly fried chicken, ready to savor the creamy coleslaw on the side. But your plate holds a surprise – a fresh salad instead.

You reach for your purse/wallet to pay at the store, but it's gone! Frantic searching reveals an empty spot in your bag. Someone must have snatched it in the crowded store. Now you have to deal with cancelled cards and a lost ID.

The stylist's comb catches on a tangle, and a yelp escapes your lips as she pulls it through. Tears well up in your eyes.

You take a celebratory bite of your juicy hamburger, ready to savor the flavor. But a shocking sight greets you – the inside is raw and bloody!

The wind whips through your hair as you hop on your bike, excited for a quick trip to the store. But as you pedal down the street, you realize you've passed the familiar convenience store turnoff.

Stepping off the bus, you glance at your phone and curse under your breath. You're nowhere near your intended destination! The bus is long gone, leaving you stranded at an unfamiliar stop.

Jennifer Tillock M.S. CCC-SLP

Navigating the Social Scene: Safety Tips for Teens

The teenage years are a whirlwind of social exploration. From hanging out with friends to attending parties and venturing out independently, these experiences are crucial for developing your identity and social skills. But amidst the fun, it's important to prioritize your safety. Here's a guide to navigating social situations with a sense of awareness and confidence:

Planning and Preparation:

- **Know Your Limits:** Be honest with yourself about your comfort level. Don't feel pressured to participate in activities that make you uneasy.
- **Buddy Up:** There's safety in numbers. Whenever possible, go out with a trusted friend or group of friends. Sharing your location and expected return time with them adds another layer of security.
- **Communication is Key:** Let your parents or guardians know where you're going, who you'll be with, and when you expect to be back. Check in with them periodically throughout the evening, especially if plans change.
- **Charge Up:** A dead phone can leave you stranded. Make sure your phone is fully charged before heading out. Consider carrying a portable charger if you'll be out for an extended period.
- **Cash Backup:** While relying on cards is convenient, it's wise to carry a small amount of cash for emergencies like needing a phone call or unexpected expenses.

Out and About:

- **Trust Your Gut:** Intuition is a powerful tool. If a situation feels off, it probably is. Don't hesitate to remove yourself from the situation or seek help from a friend or trusted adult.
- **Be Wary of Strangers:** Limit interaction with people you don't know. If someone approaches you and makes you uncomfortable, be assertive. Excuse yourself politely and move away.
- **Mind Your Surroundings:** Stay alert and aware of your surroundings. Avoid walking alone in poorly lit areas or secluded environments. If you're using public transportation, sit near others and avoid getting lost in your phone.

- **Be Picky About Rides:** Only accept rides from trusted sources like parents, guardians, or pre-arranged carpools. If attending a party, ensure a designated driver is available or discuss a safe ride home beforehand.

Parties and Events:

- **Know the Host:** If attending a party at someone's house, make sure it's with a friend who knows the host or at least knows someone else who will be there.
- **Assess the Atmosphere:** When you arrive, take a moment to get a feel for the environment. Is it overcrowded? Is alcohol or drug use present? If something feels wrong, don't be afraid to leave.
- **Pace Yourself:** If alcohol is served, be extremely cautious. Peer pressure can be strong, but remember, it's your body and your choice. Pace yourself, alternate alcoholic drinks with water, and know your limits.
- **Watch Out for Your Friends:** Look out for your friends and vice versa. Keep an eye on each other and ensure everyone is safe and comfortable.
- **Know Your Exit Strategy:** Have a plan for leaving the event. Arrange for a pre-determined pick-up time with your parents or friends, or consider using a ride-sharing service if safe and reliable.
- **Keep your drink safe:** Keep an eye on your drink at all times. Be aware of the risk of drink spiking, where someone adds drugs or other substances to your drink without your knowledge. Avoid accepting drinks from strangers or people you don't trust completely. Consider opting for bottled or canned drinks that you can open yourself.

Date Night Do's and Don'ts:

- **Meet in Public:** Arrange first dates for public places during daylight hours. Let someone know where you're going and your expected return time.
- **Go With Your Gut:** If something feels off, it probably is. Don't be afraid to end the date early and call a trusted friend or family member for a ride home.
- **Communicate Clearly:** Discuss boundaries and expectations beforehand. Be clear about what you're comfortable with and don't be afraid to say no.
- **Keep Finances Separate:** Avoid situations where you feel pressured to pay for everything or rely on your date for transportation home.
- **Trust Your Ride:** Only get into vehicles with people you know and trust. Consider arranging your own transportation beforehand if needed.

Unexpected Situations:

- **Lost or Separated:** If you get separated from your friends, stay calm. Try to retrace your steps or find a landmark to orient yourself. If in a building, ask security or staff for help.
- **Feeling Unwell:** If you start feeling unwell, whether due to illness, an allergic reaction, or too much alcohol, don't hesitate to tell a friend or trusted adult. Seek medical attention if necessary.

Jennifer Tillock M.S. CCC-SLP

- **Witnessing Conflict:** If you witness a conflict escalating, avoid intervening directly. Alert a security guard or trusted adult to handle the situation.
- **Harassment or Bullying:** If you experience harassment or bullying, don't suffer in silence. Report it to a friend, trusted adult, or event organizer. Take steps to remove yourself from the situation and document what happened if needed.

Developing Assertiveness:

- **Body Language:** Stand tall with good posture. Maintain eye contact while speaking and avoid fidgeting. This conveys confidence and self-assuredness.
- **Clear Communication:** Speak clearly and directly. Don't be afraid to say "no" if you're uncomfortable or pressured into something you don't want to do.
- **Set Boundaries:** It's okay to set boundaries with friends and acquaintances. Let them know what you're comfortable with and what's off-limits.

Remember:

Safety First: Never compromise your safety for peer pressure or the sake of fitting in.

Mastering the Art of Self-Advocacy: A Teen's Guide to Social Confidence

The teenage years are a social rollercoaster. From navigating friendships to juggling parties and first dates, navigating the social scene requires both confidence and self-awareness. Self-advocacy, the ability to speak up for yourself and express your needs, is a critical skill that empowers you to navigate these experiences while staying true to yourself.

This guide equips you with the tools to become a master of self-advocacy in social situations. Learn how to communicate effectively, set boundaries, and handle uncomfortable situations with grace and assertiveness.

Knowing Your Worth:

The foundation of self-advocacy is a strong sense of self-worth. Before you can effectively communicate your needs to others, you need to be clear about them yourself. Here's where some introspection comes in:

- **Identify Your Values:** What's important to you? Is it honesty, kindness, respect, or spending quality time with friends? Understanding your core values helps you make informed decisions and guide your interactions with others.
- **Recognize Your Strengths and Weaknesses:** Everyone has a unique set of talents and areas for improvement. Owning your strengths builds confidence while acknowledging your weaknesses allows you to seek support or work on self-improvement.

- **Embrace Your Uniqueness:** Don't try to fit into a mold. Celebrate your individuality and the things that make you special. Surrounding yourself with people who appreciate you for who you are allows you to thrive.

Communicate with Confidence:

Effectively expressing yourself is key to self-advocacy. Here are some tips for clear and confident communication:

- **Use "I" Statements:** When expressing needs or concerns, use "I" statements to avoid blame or accusations. For example, "I feel uncomfortable when..." is more effective than "You always..."
- **Maintain Eye Contact:** Eye contact shows confidence and interest in the conversation. However, it's okay to look away briefly to gather your thoughts or avoid being overly intense.
- **Speak Clearly and Calmy:** Even when you're upset, prioritize clear and calm communication. Shouting or speaking in a monotone will likely not yield the desired outcome.

Setting Healthy Boundaries:

Boundaries are essential for healthy relationships. They define what you're comfortable with and what's off-limits. Here's how to establish and maintain boundaries:

- **Know Your Limits:** Identify your physical, emotional, and social boundaries. For example, are you okay with staying out late? Do you enjoy physical displays of affection?
- **Communicate Clearly:** Don't expect others to read your mind. Tell your friends and family what you're comfortable with and what kind of behavior makes you feel uncomfortable.
- **Learn to Say No:** Saying no isn't rude; it's a sign of self-respect. Whether it's declining an invitation you're not interested in or refusing to participate in something that violates your boundaries, practice saying no with confidence.

Mastering Uncomfortable Situations:

Social situations don't always go as planned. Here's how to handle uncomfortable situations with self-advocacy:

- **De-escalate When Necessary:** If you're in a heated argument or a situation feels unsafe, prioritize de-escalating the situation. Remove yourself from the conversation, take deep breaths, and address the issue when emotions have calmed down.
- **Don't Be Afraid to Walk Away:** You don't have to put up with disrespect or participate in activities that make you feel uncomfortable. Have the courage to walk away from a situation if it violates your boundaries.
- **Seek Support:** If you're struggling with a complex situation, don't hesitate to seek help from a trusted adult, friend, or therapist. Support networks can offer valuable advice and help you navigate these challenges.

Remember:

Self-advocacy is a journey, not a destination. It takes time and practice to become comfortable communicating your needs and asserting yourself. Don't be discouraged by setbacks. Celebrate your victories and keep practicing!

The Takeaway:

By embracing self-advocacy, you empower yourself to thrive in social settings. You learn to express yourself clearly, set healthy boundaries, and navigate difficult situations with confidence. Remember, it's okay to say no, prioritize your well-being, and surround yourself with people who respect you for who you are.

Scenarios

You witness a bullying incident online targeting a classmate. Knowing it's wrong, you grapple with the decision to intervene and speak up to defend the victim while navigating the potential for online conflict.

You're at a party with a large punch bowl. Everyone seems to be grabbing cups and filling them, but you notice people leaving theirs unattended on a nearby table. You haven't seen your friends in a while, and you're starting to feel a little thirsty.

You're on a date with someone new. They offer to buy you a drink, but you only see unfamiliar craft beers on tap. They suggest trying a mixed drink they "know you'll love." You're curious, but something about the situation makes you feel uneasy.

You're hanging out with a group of friends after school. Someone suggests going to a new club you've never been to before. You're not familiar with the area, and you know it'll likely be crowded. While you want to have fun with your friends, you're also worried about feeling overwhelmed and unsafe in an unknown environment.

You're at a concert with your best friend. The mosh pit is getting wild, and you're starting to feel jostled and uncomfortable. Your friend seems to be having a blast, but you're worried about getting hurt or separated from them in the crowd.

You're studying with a group for a big test tomorrow. One person in the group keeps trying to change the subject and talk about something else. You feel like you're not getting much studying done, and you're worried about being unprepared for the test.

You're in class and the teacher announces a surprise pop quiz. You haven't been keeping up with the readings lately, and you know you won't do well. You feel a pang of anxiety, but you also know you deserve a fair chance to show what you've learned.

You're at a job interview, and the interviewer asks you a question that you don't feel fully prepared to answer. You want to make a good impression, but you also don't want to give an inaccurate or misleading response.

You're on a school trip, and you're partnered with someone you don't know well on a group project. They seem to be taking charge and making most of the decisions without asking for your input. You have some great ideas to contribute, but you're worried about speaking up.

You're at the mall with a friend, and you see a cool jacket you really want to try on. The problem is, it's a bit out of your price range. You don't want to disappoint your friend if you can't afford it, but you also don't want to spend money you don't have.

The music thumps, the strobe lights flash. You reach for your drink on the crowded dance floor, only to find it empty. A stranger beside you offers a colorful concoction from a mysterious flask tucked in their jacket. You hesitate, unsure how long it's been out or what's in it.

You're at a party with a new group. They pressure you to try the brightly colored punch, but you notice it's been left unattended for a while. An unsettling feeling creeps in, and you wonder if it's safe.

Your date suggests going for a walk after dinner, but the path leads towards a secluded part of the park. You voice your hesitation, wanting to stay in a well-lit area with more people around.

Your study partner at the library starts making suggestive comments that make you feel uneasy. You don't want to cause a scene, but you also don't want things to go any further.

You're out with friends, and you need to use the restroom. They're all crammed together in a spot with limited visibility. You consider your options, wanting some company to ensure your safety.

You bump into an acquaintance at a party. They offer you a drink they brought themself, but you haven't seen them all night and can't be sure where the drink came from. You appreciate the gesture, but something feels off.

You're on a date that's taken a turn. Your date starts pressuring you for physical intimacy, making you feel increasingly uncomfortable. You try to communicate your boundaries, wanting to make it clear you're not interested.

You're at a concert with a large group. The crowd gets rowdy, and you get separated from your friends. Panic starts to rise as you feel alone in the throng of people.

You're chilling with friends by a bonfire. Someone offers a mysterious drink they keep hidden in their jacket. The situation feels strange, and you don't recognize the drink. You want to politely decline, unsure of the potential risk.

Your date orders another round of drinks at the bar. You watch as they turn away for a moment to chat with the bartender. Although you trust them, a recent news story about drugged drinks comes to mind. You wrestle with a decision, wanting to ensure your safety.

You're scrolling through social media and see a friend post something that makes fun of another classmate. You know this kind of online bullying can be hurtful, and you're not sure if you should say something.

Butterflies flutter in your stomach – you just scored your first date! You're excited to meet your date at the coffee shop, but a slight hitch arises. They text you, suggesting they pick you up at your house instead. You've only interacted online, and getting into a car with someone new makes you uneasy.

Scrolling through social media with your date, a post about splitting the cost of concert tickets catches your eye. Suddenly, your date mentions expecting you to "contribute" to the evening's activities. Caught off guard, you realize you weren't aware of this expectation, and you might not have enough cash on hand for your share.

The conversation flows easily as you chat with your date over dinner. Suddenly, their phone buzzes, and they're captivated by the screen. Throughout the meal, their attention bounces between you and their social media feed, making you feel a little ignored. You want to enjoy the date in person, not compete with their online world.

The meal is delicious, and conversation is pleasant. Your date suggests taking a walk along a scenic trail after dinner. As the sun dips below the horizon, casting long shadows, you hesitate. The secluded area feels a bit deserted, and you're not comfortable being alone with someone you just met, especially in the growing darkness.

Your date punctuates their jokes with humor that targets specific groups of people. While you appreciate lightheartedness, their comments feel disrespectful and demeaning. You don't want to be associated with those views and feel a pang of discomfort.

Holding hands can be a sweet part of getting to know someone, but you're not quite ready for that level of physical contact yet. During the movie, your date reaches for your hand, their fingers brushing against yours. You respect their feelings, but you want to take things at your own pace.

Your date excitedly talks about an upcoming party with their friends. They casually mention

expecting you to be their plus one. You haven't even met their friends yet, and the idea of being introduced to a whole new group feels overwhelming. You'd like to take things slower and get to know your date better before attending social gatherings together.

Dating can be exciting, but sometimes the conversation takes an unexpected turn. Your date keeps dwelling on their recent breakup, recounting the drama in detail. The conversation feels heavy, and you'd rather focus on getting to know each other in a more positive light.

Browsing social media after your date, you come across a surprise – a picture of you and your date posted publicly. While the gesture might seem sweet, you feel a pang of discomfort. You haven't gotten to know your date well yet, and you're not comfortable with your image being shared online without your permission.

A few dates in, you realize you're not feeling a romantic spark with your partner. You appreciate their company, but you don't see a future together.

You're invited to a party by a classmate you don't know well. Unsure of the potential social dynamics, you navigate between wanting to expand your social circle and feeling comfortable in the environment.

You're at a party with a large group you're not familiar with. The conversation lulls, and you feel a bit awkward standing alone. Wanting to connect with others but unsure how to break into established groups, you consider initiating conversation with someone new.

Jennifer Tillock M.S. CCC-SLP

You're enjoying a game of charades at a party when you're assigned a word you're unfamiliar with. Feeling frustrated and embarrassed that you might slow down the game, you hesitate to ask for clarification. However, you also don't want to perform a charade that nobody understands.

You're at a party where a group gathers around a table playing a complex board game. While you're interested in joining in on the fun, you haven't played the game before and worry you might slow down the gameplay or make mistakes.

The party host announces there will be a dance competition later in the evening. You're not a confident dancer and feel self-conscious about participating in front of others. However, you also don't want to miss out on the fun and camaraderie of the competition.

You're at a party with a friend who starts telling an embarrassing story about you in front of a group of people. While the story is meant to be humorous, you feel uncomfortable with the details being shared publicly.

You arrive at a party and realize you forgot to bring gum or mints. You typically chew gum after eating to freshen your breath, but you're unsure if it's appropriate to ask the party host if they have any to spare. You feel really self-conscious about bad breath.

The party atmosphere is loud and crowded. You're enjoying the music but starting to feel overwhelmed by the noise and lack of personal space. Knowing you need a break to avoid sensory overload, you consider different ways to excuse yourself for a short while without seeming rude.

You're at a party where a group gathers around a bonfire outdoors. While you enjoy the warmth and ambiance of the fire, the smoke irritates your eyes and makes it difficult to breathe. However, you don't want to be the only person standing far away from the fire.

Your best friend comes to your house and asks to spend the night, but doesn't want your parents to know. You're torn. You love sleepovers with your best friend, but disobeying your parents' rules makes you uncomfortable.

You are having a sleepover and your friend brings alcohol. This situation raises a red flag. Alcohol is dangerous for minors, and you're worried about the potential consequences of underage drinking.

You are with your friends and they are laughing at something mean they said to someone online. Cyberbullying is a serious issue, and you feel uncomfortable with your friends' behavior.

Your friend always calls you a dork. They are just joking, but it still hurts your feelings. Even if meant playfully, constant teasing can be hurtful.

You go to your locker at the end of the day and there are two kids in front of it, starting a fight. Seeing a fight break out is scary.

You use your allowance to buy makeup. Your sister keeps using it without asking. Sharing is important, but you also want to protect your belongings.

Your friend really enjoys outdoor activities, but you sunburn easily, even with sunscreen. You don't want to miss out on spending time with your friend, but you also need to protect your skin.

You think your friend might be in trouble and need help. Seeing a friend struggle can be tough. You can try talking to them directly and offering your support.

You're playing a game of truth or dare at a party. You land on "dare" and the person who dares you asks you to do something silly that makes you feel uncomfortable.

A friend at the party offers you a slice of homemade cake. You have a nut allergy and avoid nuts in your diet altogether. However, you don't want to offend your friend by refusing the offered dessert, especially if they made it themselves.

At a friend's party, the atmosphere shifts. People are pressuring you to participate in activities that make you uncomfortable. You want to have fun, but you also want to feel safe and respected. Figuring out how to navigate the situation without causing drama becomes your biggest challenge.

At a crowded party, you witness someone spiking another person's drink. Intervention feels risky, but so does walking away and pretending you didn't see anything. A difficult choice hangs in the air.

A classmate you barely know asks to borrow your expensive headphones. You worry about them coming back damaged, but you don't want to seem unfriendly. The decision to trust or not leaves you hesitant.

Your new outfit arrives! The package is marked delivered, but nowhere to be found. Stolen or misplaced? You contemplate telling your parents or trying to handle it yourself.

You're coerced by a friend to participate in a risky activity that makes you uncomfortable. Pressure mounts as you navigate how to say no while maintaining the friendship.

Hanging out at the park, a friend whips out a vape pen, offering it around. You know the risks of underage vaping, but fear of being left out clouds your judgment. Pressure to take a puff makes you pause, unsure what to do.

You're hanging out with a friend at their house, and their parents offer you alcohol. You don't want to drink, but you don't want to seem lame either.

You loaned your bright pink phone charger with the cute cat ears attached to your friend Jessica a week ago. You really need it back now because your phone battery is about to die, and you have an important project due tomorrow.

Your friends excitedly announce they're planning a weekend trip to the new arcade downtown, boasting about all the high-score games they'll conquer. You secretly dread going – you know you can't afford to spend money on games, and you worry you'll just stand around awkwardly while they play.

You planned to hang out with your friend Michael after school. When he pulls up in his sleek motorcycle, your heart sinks. He only has one helmet, and you never agreed to ride without proper safety gear. The cool afternoon breeze feels enticing, but the potential danger makes you uneasy.

You're at a party thrown by a classmate you barely know. The loud music and unfamiliar faces make you feel a little on edge. You grab a refreshing cup of soda, but nature calls.

It's a scorching summer day, and your friends suggest cooling off with a trip to your favorite ice cream shop. Unfortunately, you're lactose intolerant and can't indulge in creamy treats.

You've noticed a shift in your friend Alex's behavior lately. The once energetic and talkative Alex has become withdrawn and quiet. They seem constantly down and avoid hanging out as much. This change concerns you, but you don't want to pry.

Lately, your friend Sarah seems constantly down. Conversations often turn towards sad topics, and she frequently mentions feeling overwhelmed. You want to be there for her, but you're not sure how to best offer support.

As you're packing your things after the final school bell rings, a classmate corners you in the hallway. He throws a menacing glare your way and mutters a chilling threat about meeting you after school for a "fight." Fear

washes over you – you've never had any problems with this person before.

You're spending time with your friend Maya, catching up on the latest gossip. As she reaches for a book on a high shelf, you notice a dark bruise peeking out from under the strap of her tank top. It concerns you – this isn't the first unexplained mark you've seen on her lately. You want to express your concern without causing offense, but you also wonder if you should intervene or encourage her to confide in someone about what's happening.

You're happily engrossed in building a giant pillow fort with the kids you're babysitting when the doorbell rings. It's your friend Alex, unexpectedly dropping by. You're torn – you were looking forward to catching up with Alex, but you also have a responsibility to the children you're caring for.

Pumped with excitement, you arrive at the stadium clutching your ticket for the prime seat you saved up for weeks to afford. Elated, you scan the row, ready to settle into the perfect view, only to find someone already comfortably occupying your designated seat. Disappointment washes over you – you paid a premium for this experience.

The music thumps, the strobe lights flash, and the party buzzes with teenage energy. You're having a great time catching up with classmates, but a few situations make you pause and consider your safety and ability to speak up for yourself.

You mingle with a group, but someone you don't recognize leans in and offers a red solo cup filled with an unknown blue liquid. "Want some punch?" they slur. You've never met this person, and their unsteady stance raises a red flag.

The party erupts in cheers as a game of "last one standing" is announced. This typically involves jumping around and bumping into others, but you remember the sprained ankle you haven't fully recovered from.

The party host, a senior you barely know, announces a beer pong tournament with the winner getting a prize. You're not interested in alcohol and never participated in beer pong before. The pressure to join builds as classmates nudge you towards the table.

Across the room, you see Sarah, a classmate, stumbling around. Her speech is slurred, and her eyes are glazed over. Concern washes over you – you know Sarah wouldn't normally act this way.

You're engrossed in conversation with a new friend, Maya, who you met earlier at the party. Suddenly, Maya mentions living across town and casually offers you a ride home. While you enjoy Maya's company, getting into a car with someone you just met feels unsafe.

The party spills outside onto the lawn, and you find yourself standing near a group huddled around a fire pit. The acrid smell of cigarette smoke stings your eyes. Secondhand smoke irritates your asthma, and you know you need to move away.

A plate of delicious-looking cookies makes its way around the party. You reach for one, but then remember your severe nut allergy. How can you politely decline the cookie and explain your allergy without seeming ungrateful or picky, especially if the cookies were homemade by the host?

The party atmosphere intensifies. The music volume escalates, and the growing crowd makes you feel overwhelmed. Anxiety starts to creep in, and you crave a quieter space to regroup.

You witness a group of classmates laughing and pointing at someone standing alone across the room. Their hurtful comments sting your ears, and you recognize the signs of bullying. Feeling uncomfortable with the situation, how can you subtly intervene and show support for the person being targeted?

The party stretches on, and you start to feel increasingly tired and out of place. Maybe you're not in the mood for the loud music anymore, or you simply don't feel like staying any longer. However, you don't want to seem like a party pooper or upset your friends who seem to be having a good time.

You're hanging out with a group of friends at someone's house. The mood is light, and conversation flows easily. Suddenly, someone pulls out a bag of pills, claiming they're just relaxation aids. You've never seen these pills before, and you're unsure of their effects.

While scrolling through social media, you see a friend posting about a new "party favor" they received. The image shows a small, brightly colored candy-like object. You've heard rumors about these "treats" containing psychoactive substances, but you're unsure if the rumors are true.

Jennifer Tillock M.S. CCC-SLP

Social

You're at a concert with a large crowd. Someone you barely know bumps into you and offers a cigarette that seems suspicious. The pungent odor is unfamiliar, and you suspect it might be laced with something stronger than tobacco.

Your friend group is planning a weekend getaway to a cabin in the woods. While discussing the trip, someone casually mentions bringing "supplies" to enhance the experience. You know this likely refers to drugs, and you're uncomfortable with the idea of being around them.

You overhear a conversation between classmates about a new vaping trend. They describe the flavors as fruity and harmless, but you're worried about the potential health risks associated with vaping.

You receive a text message from a friend asking if you want to "chill" at their place after school. You know this is often code for using drugs, and you don't want to be involved.

You're at a party and witness someone pressuring another person to take a drink from a mysterious flask. The situation feels tense, and you're worried about the person being pressured.

You're at a sporting event with a group of friends. During halftime, you notice someone in your group acting strangely. Their behavior seems erratic, and their speech is slurred. You suspect they might have taken something, and you're concerned for their safety.

A friend confides in you that they're experimenting with drugs to cope with stress. You care about your friend and want to help, but you're unsure how to navigate this sensitive situation.

The party's energy is infectious, but you're starting to feel drained. You glance at your friend Sarah, who's having a blast dancing with a new group. You promised your parents you'd be home by midnight, and the clock is ticking closer.

The pulsing music and flashing lights make you realize you desperately need a bathroom break. However, you remember the warnings about leaving drinks unattended at parties. Your brightly colored cup with the cute cat straw sits precariously on a crowded table. Leaving it behind feels risky, but so does holding it precariously while navigating the throng of people or taking it into the bathroom.

Across the room, a boy you like winks at you and gestures towards the stairs leading to the upper floor of the house. His intentions are unclear, but a shiver runs down your spine. You don't feel comfortable following him upstairs, especially to a secluded area.

Medical and Mental Safety Tips: Navigating Your Health with Confidence

Your teenage years are a whirlwind of growth, change, and exploration. It's also a time when you're taking more responsibility for your own health and well-being. This can feel overwhelming at times, but being informed about medical and mental safety can empower you to make smart choices and navigate challenges effectively. Here are some key areas to keep in mind:

Physical Health:

- **Listen to your body:** It's your best communication tool. Pay attention to aches, pains, changes in energy levels, or unusual sleep patterns. These can be early signs of illness, injury, or stress.

- **Fuel your body wisely:** Teenagers need a balanced diet rich in fruits, vegetables, whole grains, and lean proteins to support growth and development. Avoid fad diets and focus on nourishing your body for optimal health.

- **Stay hydrated:** Water is essential for every bodily function. Aim to carry a reusable water bottle and sip throughout the day, especially during physical activity or hot weather.

- **Move your body:** Exercise is crucial for physical and mental health. Find activities you enjoy, whether it's team sports, dancing, hiking, or simply taking a brisk walk. Aim for at least 30 minutes of moderate-intensity exercise most days of the week.

- **Get enough sleep:** Teenagers typically need 8-10 hours of sleep each night. A regular sleep schedule promotes concentration, mood regulation, and physical recovery.

- **Practice good hygiene:** Wash your hands frequently, especially before eating, after using the bathroom, or after being in public spaces. This helps prevent the spread of germs and illness.

- **Protect your skin:** Sun exposure can be damaging. Apply sunscreen with SPF 30 or higher daily, even on cloudy days. Wear protective clothing like hats and sunglasses when spending time outdoors.

- **Know your family history:** Talk to your parents about any medical conditions that run in your family. This information can be helpful for early detection and preventive measures.

- **Schedule regular checkups:** Don't wait until you feel sick to see a doctor. Regular checkups allow your doctor to monitor your health and identify any potential problems early on.

- **Be informed about healthy relationships:** Learn to recognize and avoid unhealthy or abusive relationships. Healthy relationships are supportive, respectful, and free from violence or manipulation.

Mental Health:

- **Recognize your emotions:** It's normal to experience a wide range of emotions. Take time to identify and acknowledge how you're feeling.

- **Develop healthy coping mechanisms:** Find healthy ways to manage stress and difficult emotions. This could include exercise, journaling, spending time in nature, listening to music, or talking to a trusted friend or family member.

- **Practice relaxation techniques:** Deep breathing exercises, meditation, and yoga can all be helpful for managing stress and anxiety.

- Build a strong support system: Surround yourself with positive and supportive people who care about your well-being.

- **Seek help when needed:** Don't be afraid to ask for help if you're struggling with your mental health. Talking to a counselor, therapist, or doctor can provide valuable support and guidance.

- **Beware of social media comparisons:** Social media often portrays an idealized version of reality. Limit your social media use and avoid comparing yourself to others.

- **Prioritize sleep:** As mentioned earlier, adequate sleep is crucial for mental well-being too. Develop a regular sleep schedule and practice good sleep hygiene for a restful night's sleep.

- **Practice mindfulness:** Mindfulness involves being present in the moment and paying attention to your thoughts and feelings without judgment. Mindfulness exercises can help you manage stress and improve your overall well-being.

- **Challenge negative thoughts:** We all have negative self-talk sometimes. Learn to recognize negative thought patterns and challenge them with positive affirmations.

Jennifer Tillock M.S. CCC-SLP

- **Celebrate your strengths and accomplishments:** Take time to appreciate your unique talents and achievements. Building self-esteem fosters mental well-being.

Substance Use and Safety:

- **Understand the risks:** Educate yourself about the dangers of drugs, alcohol, and tobacco use. These substances can have a significant impact on your physical and mental health, academic performance, and relationships.

- **Peer pressure can be strong:** Develop healthy refusal skills to resist peer pressure to engage in risky activities. A simple "no thanks" or "I'm not interested" is perfectly acceptable.

- **Be aware of your surroundings:** Never leave a drink unattended at a party or social event. There's a risk of someone adding drugs or alcohol without your knowledge.

- **Seek help if needed:** If you or someone you know is struggling with substance abuse, don't hesitate to seek help. There are many resources available, including hotlines, support groups, and treatment centers.

Safety and Injury Prevention:

- **Be aware of your surroundings:** Pay attention to your environment and potential hazards. This includes avoiding distractions like your phone while walking or biking.

- **Use safety equipment:** Always wear appropriate safety gear for activities like bike helmets, knee pads, or goggles, depending on the activity.

- **Practice safe driving:** If you're old enough to drive, follow traffic laws, avoid distractions, and never drive under the influence of alcohol or drugs.

- **Sun safety:** In addition to sunscreen, wear protective clothing and seek shade, especially during peak sun hours (10 am to 4 pm)

- Fire safety: Learn about fire safety protocols at home and school. Know the location of fire extinguishers and escape routes in case of an emergency.

- **Water safety:** Never swim alone and always supervise younger children around water. Be aware of your limits and only swim in designated areas.

- **Be informed about first aid:** Learn basic first aid skills like CPR and how to treat minor injuries.

- **Know your emergency contacts:** Have important phone numbers readily available, such as your parents, doctor, and emergency services.

- **Trust your gut:** If a situation feels unsafe, it probably is. Remove yourself from the situation and seek help from a trusted adult.

Additional Resources:

This information is a starting point, and there are many resources available to help you learn more about specific health and safety topics. Here are some helpful resources:

- **Your doctor:** Your doctor is a valuable resource for all your health concerns. Don't hesitate to ask questions or express any worries you may have.

- **School nurse**: The school nurse can address any immediate health concerns and provide information about healthy habits.

- **Mental health resources**: Many schools offer access to counselors or therapists who can provide support for mental health challenges.

- **National hotlines:** Hotlines like the National Suicide Prevention Lifeline (1-800-273-8255) or the Crisis Text Line (text HOME to 741741) can offer immediate support in times of crisis.

- **Reliable websites:** Government websites like the Centers for Disease Control and Prevention (CDC) or the National Institute of Mental Health (NIMH) offer trustworthy information on various health topics.

Remember: Taking charge of your health and safety is empowering. By making informed choices and seeking help when needed, you can navigate your teenage years with confidence and build a foundation for a healthy and fulfilling life.

Medical and Mental Health Self-Advocacy for Teens: Your Voice Matters

Being a teenager involves a gradual shift from relying on parents to manage your health to taking more responsibility for your well-being. This includes advocating for yourself in medical and mental health settings. Self-advocacy empowers you to communicate your needs and concerns effectively, ensuring you receive the best possible care. Here are some key strategies to develop your self-advocacy skills:

Preparation is Key:

- **Gather information:** Before any doctor's appointment, write down your symptoms, questions, and any medications you're taking. Researching your condition online from reliable websites like the Mayo Clinic or the National Institutes of Health can also be helpful, but remember, it shouldn't replace professional guidance.

- **Organize your thoughts:** Jot down key points you want to discuss with the doctor. This helps you stay focused and ensures you don't forget anything important during the appointment.

Jennifer Tillock M.S. CCC-SLP

- **Bring a support person:** Consider bringing a parent, trusted friend, or family member to accompany you to appointments. They can offer moral support, take notes, and help you remember details later.

Communication is Crucial:

- **Be clear and concise:** Clearly state your symptoms, concerns, and any questions you have. Speak up if you don't understand something the doctor is explaining.

- **Use "I" statements:** Expressing yourself with "I" statements takes ownership of your feelings and concerns. For example, "I've been feeling tired lately, and it's affecting my schoolwork," is more impactful than simply saying, "I'm tired."

- **Ask clarifying questions:** Don't hesitate to ask for clarification if you don't understand the doctor's explanation. Rephrase their instructions or ask them to break things down into simpler terms.

- **Be assertive, not aggressive:** There's a difference between being assertive and aggressive. State your needs clearly and confidently, but remain respectful towards the medical professional.

Understanding Your Options:

- **Discuss treatment options:** Ask the doctor to explain different treatment options available to you. Inquire about the benefits and potential side effects of each course of action.

- **Seek second opinions:** If you're unsure about a diagnosis or treatment plan, don't hesitate to seek a second opinion from another healthcare professional. This can give you peace of mind and a broader perspective on your health.

- **Express your preferences:** You have a right to express your preferences regarding treatment. Discuss any concerns you have and work collaboratively with the doctor to find a plan that fits your needs and lifestyle.

Mental Health Self-Advocacy:

- **Normalize seeking help:** Debunk the stigma surrounding mental health by openly discussing the importance of seeking help when needed. Talking to a counselor or therapist is a sign of strength, not weakness.

- **Identify your needs:** Reflect on the challenges you're facing and what kind of support would be most beneficial. Do you need someone to talk to, coping mechanisms for stress, or medication management?

- **Be transparent with your therapist:** The therapeutic relationship thrives on honesty. Be open and honest with your therapist about your thoughts, feelings, and any past experiences that might be impacting your mental health.

- **Ask questions about therapy:** If you're unsure about any aspect of therapy, don't hesitate to ask your therapist for clarification. Understanding the process and goals of therapy can enhance your comfort level and participation.

- **Track your progress:** Keep a journal or create a mood tracker to monitor your progress over time. This can be helpful in identifying patterns, celebrating improvements, and adjusting your treatment plan as needed.

Building Confidence:

- **Research your rights:** Educate yourself about your rights as a patient. Knowing your rights empowers you to make informed decisions about your healthcare.

- **Practice assertive communication:** Role-play conversations with a trusted friend or family member to practice speaking up for yourself clearly and confidently.

- **Celebrate your successes:** Acknowledge your progress when you successfully advocate for yourself. This reinforces your self-confidence and motivates you to continue speaking up for your well-being.

Additional Tips:

- **Don't be afraid to say no:** You have the right to refuse any treatment option you're uncomfortable with. Don't feel pressured to agree to something you don't understand or fully support.

- **Bring a list of medications:** Maintain a list of all medications you're taking, including over-the-counter drugs and supplements. Keep the list updated and bring it to every medical appointment.

- **Know your family history:** Being aware of any health conditions that run in your family can be helpful for early detection and preventive measures. Talk to your parents and gather information about any relevant family health history.

- **Find a doctor you trust:** Having a good rapport with your doctor is crucial for effective communication and self-advocacy. If you don't feel comfortable with your current doctor, consider seeking a new one who listens attentively to your concerns and involves you in the decision-making process.

- **Utilize online resources:** Many credible websites offer information on medical conditions, healthy habits, and mental health resources. These online resources can empower you to learn more about your health and self-advocate for your well-being.

Remember: Self-advocacy is a skill that takes time and practice to develop. Don't get discouraged if you don't feel completely confident at first. Keep practicing, seeking support from trusted adults, and celebrating your progress. By taking charge of your health and mental well-being, you're building a foundation for a healthy and empowered future.

Jennifer Tillock M.S. CCC-SLP

Scenarios

You're at the dermatologist's office for a mole check. The doctor points out a spot that requires further examination. You are feeling overwhelmed and a little scared.

Sitting in the dentist's chair, the hygienist starts cleaning your teeth. The pressure feels uncomfortable, and your gums begin to bleed a little. Unsure if this is normal, how will you communicate your discomfort and ask the hygienist to be gentler during the cleaning?

Browsing online forums, you stumble upon a website promoting a "miracle" weight loss supplement. The claims seem too good to be true, and the flashy graphics raise suspicion.

During a routine eye exam, the optometrist places drops in your eyes to dilate your pupils. However, you experience a burning sensation and your vision becomes blurry.

You're struggling with a new medication that has unpleasant side effects. It makes you so dizzy you have a hard time navigating the school building.

You notice your friend constantly engaging in risky behaviors, like sneaking out late at night or experimenting with drugs. Their thrill-seeking tendencies worry you, and you debate how to express your concern without seeming judgmental.

A friend opens up to you about self-harming behaviors as a way to cope with difficult emotions. This revelation comes as a shock, and you feel a mix of fear and empathy.

You suspect your friend might be struggling with an eating disorder. They've become secretive about their eating habits, and you've noticed them skipping meals or making excuses about what they've eaten. You're worried about their physical and mental health.

You witness your friend experiencing intense anxiety before a big presentation or social event. They become physically shaky, have trouble catching their breath, and seem paralyzed by fear. You want to offer support but aren't sure if calming reassurances are enough.

A friend confides in you about feeling depressed. They express a lack of interest in activities they used to enjoy, isolate themselves, and have lost their usual energy and enthusiasm. You're concerned about their well-being and want to encourage them to seek help.

You're helping your parents clean the garage and discover a box of old medication. Curious about what they are, you consider taking some to see what they do.

You open the bottle of your refilled allergy medication and frown. The pills are a different color and shape than what you're used to. Uncertainty washes over you.

You're applying eyeliner, trying to get that perfect wing, when you miscalculate and jab the tip of the pencil right into your eye. Tears well up, and your vision goes blurry. Even after a minute of rinsing with water, your eye still stings fiercely.

You're home alone with your younger brother when he trips and falls, hitting his head hard on the coffee table. He lies motionless, and you can't rouse him.

You're enjoying lunch in the crowded cafeteria when a piece of chicken gets lodged in your throat. You gasp, unable to breathe. Panic sets in as you clutch your throat, silently struggling for air.

Stepping out of a relaxing bath, your foot hits a wet spot on the floor, sending you sprawling. Your head cracks against the edge of the tub, and a wave of dizziness washes over you.

You glance at your scraped knee from a soccer game a few days ago. It's gotten noticeably red, swollen, and is even oozing some pus. You wonder if it's infected.

You take your daily medication for asthma every morning, but as you brush your teeth, a nagging doubt creeps in. Did you already take it, or are you imagining it? You can't quite recall.

You signed in to the doctor's office 30 minutes ago, and the lady that signed in after you is called. It is 20 minutes past your appointment.

You wake up in the middle of the night feeling unwell. You're unsure if you should wake your parents or try to tough it out until morning.

You're stressed about an upcoming exam and can't seem to focus on studying. You consider taking a "study aid" someone at school mentioned.

You're getting ready in the morning and reach for your allergy medication. But the cabinet is dark and you accidentally grab the wrong bottle. You take a dose before realizing it's not your medication.

You've been feeling down lately. Everything seems overwhelming, and even getting out of bed takes a ton of effort. Tears come easily, and you can't pinpoint why you feel this way. You know something isn't right.

While reaching for a glass in the cabinet, you lose your footing and slam your face into the door. Your lip throbs and you taste blood. A chipped tooth wobbles precariously in your mouth.

You're absentmindedly curling your hair when the iron touches your finger for a beat too long. The searing pain is immediate, and you pull your hand back with a yelp. A red welt starts to form on your skin, and you worry about the severity of the burn.

Helping your mom with dinner, you carry a steaming pot of noodles to the sink. Suddenly, you trip, sending the boiling water cascading down your stomach and legs. The scalding pain is excruciating, and you scream for help, unsure of the extent of the burns.

Jennifer Tillock M.S. CCC-SLP

You're hanging out at a friend's house when they offer you some pills. Unsure of what they are, you politely decline. Later, you notice your friend acting strangely, lethargic and sweating. They confess they took some pills they found at home, but are now scared to tell their parents.

You're home alone, relaxing on the couch, when a wave of dizziness washes over you. Your heart starts pounding, and you feel faint. The room starts to spin, and you struggle to catch your breath.

You're spending the night at a friend's house. Everything is going great until your friend suddenly gasps and clutches their throat. Their face turns pale, and they're struggling to breathe.

You struggle with the weight of your overloaded backpack, finally managing to heave it onto your shoulders. Relief washes over you momentarily, but then a searing pain explodes in your toes. You wiggle your foot gingerly, but the throbbing is intense. An hour later, the swelling hasn't subsided, and you worry a simple backpack mishap might have caused a more serious injury.

Helping your dad with yard work, you misjudge a swing of the axe while trimming a branch. A sharp crack splits the air as the thick branch slams into your head. Stars cloud your vision, and a dull ache throbs where the impact occurred. You feel disoriented and fuzzy.

Everything feels pointless lately. School, friends, even hobbies – none of it seems to spark any joy. A crushing weight of hopelessness settles on you, and the thought of simply giving up whispers in your mind. You know these feelings aren't normal, but shame and fear prevent you from reaching out for help.

You're roughhousing with a friend when you take a tumble and hit your head hard on the floor. Stars dance in your vision, and a dull ache spreads across your head. The throbbing intensifies, and nausea starts to rise.

You're playing video games with your younger brother when his body suddenly stiffens. His head snaps back, and his limbs begin to jerk uncontrollably. Fear grips you as you witness what appears to be a seizure. You've never seen anything like it before.

You're pushing yourself during a workout, determined to improve your endurance. Suddenly, you're struck by a wave of dizziness. Your vision starts to tunnel, and your body wracks with uncontrollable tremors.

A stubborn nosebleed disrupts your day. You pinch your nose and lean forward, hoping the flow of blood will stop. But after 30 agonizing minutes, the bright red stream continues to trickle down your face.

You're relaxing at home with your grandma when you notice a change in her. Her speech becomes slurred and difficult to understand. Her face seems uneven, with one side drooping slightly. A pit of fear forms in your stomach.

Lately, dizziness has become a constant companion. Even simple activities like studying or reading send the room spinning. The disorientation disrupts your daily routine.

You're helping prepare dinner, carefully chopping vegetables. Suddenly, the knife slips, slicing across your finger. Blood wells up quickly, and despite applying pressure and a bandage, the bleeding continues unabated. The sight of the persistent blood flow worries you.

While prepping dinner, you accidentally nick your finger with the knife. The cut is shallow and barely bleeds.

You were organizing your closet and needed to reach something high up. Grasping the ladder, you ascend carefully, but misjudge the final step. The world lurches beneath you, and you land with a thud, hitting your head hard on the floor. Stars dance in your vision, and a wave of dizziness washes over you. Panic sets in as you realize you'll be home alone for a few hours.

Sizzling and the enticing aroma of dinner fill the kitchen as you cook. Reaching for a spatula, you accidentally brush your hand against the hot surface of the pan. A searing pain explodes on your skin, and you quickly pull your hand back. A red welt instantly forms on your contact point, and within minutes, a painful blister develops.

You're at a sleepover and wake up in the night feeling unwell. Your stomach is cramping, and you think you're running a fever.

During gym class, you injure your ankle during a jump. The pain is sharp, and you can't put any weight on it. You are embarrassed to mention it in front of your friends.

You notice a suspicious rash developing on your arm. It's itchy and spreading, and you're worried it might be something contagious.

You're working on a science project that requires using some household chemicals. The safety instructions seem complicated, and you're unsure if you fully understand the risks involved. You don't want to ask for help and seem unprepared, but you also prioritize your safety and well-being while conducting the experiment.

You notice a change in your friend's behavior. They're becoming increasingly secretive and spending time with a new group you don't know well.

Your friend confides in you that they're struggling with an eating disorder. They haven't told anyone else, and you're unsure how to best support them. You want to encourage them to seek help but don't want to judge or pressure them in a way that pushes them further away.

You're hanging out with a friend who constantly seems tired and withdrawn. They mention they're having trouble sleeping but are hesitant to talk to their parents about it.

A friend pressures you to join them in trying a new vaping product. You're unsure of the health risks and uncomfortable with inhaling unknown substances.

Jennifer Tillock M.S. CCC-SLP

The weather is scorching hot, everyone's sporting tank tops and shorts, but your friend starts wearing long sleeves every time you hang out. You casually inquire if they're feeling chilly, but they brush it off.

Lunchtime with your friend used to be a social affair filled with chatter and shared bites. Lately, however, they consistently decline food, claiming they're not hungry or already ate beforehand. Their persistent lack of appetite at meals together worries you.

Going out with your friend used to involve them devouring their food with gusto. Now, they order meals like everyone else, but the conversation and laughter take center stage as they barely touch their plate. You watch them push food around suspiciously.

Trips to the bathroom after meals have become a regular occurrence with your friend. They excuse themselves immediately after eating, returning flushed and seemingly relieved. Their frequent and hurried bathroom visits after meals spark concern.

A close friend confides in you that they're feeling overwhelmed with schoolwork and extracurricular activities. They haven't slept well in weeks and seem constantly on the verge of tears. You're concerned about their stress levels.

You overhear your friend talking negatively about themselves, focusing on perceived flaws and failures. They constantly compare themselves to others and seem to struggle with self-esteem. You want to offer support but aren't sure if pointing out their negativity will be helpful.

Your friend starts isolating themselves from the group, preferring to spend time alone in their room. They seem withdrawn and disinterested in usual activities. You're concerned about their sudden change in behavior.

Jennifer Tillock M.S. CCC-SLP

Driving

Hitting the Road: A Guide to Safe Driving and Self-Advocacy for Teens

Getting your driver's license is a milestone that unlocks a new level of freedom. But with that freedom comes a big responsibility: keeping yourself and others safe on the road. This guide equips you with essential driving and vehicle safety tips, along with self-advocacy strategies to navigate situations where you might need to speak up for yourself.

Mastering the Basics:

- **Knowledge is Power:** Before getting behind the wheel, thoroughly study your state's traffic laws and driving regulations. Understand road signs, right-of-way rules, and safe driving practices in various weather conditions.

- **Practice Makes Perfect:** Don't jump straight into highway driving. Get plenty of practice in controlled environments like empty parking lots or quiet residential streets with a licensed adult supervising you.

- **Buckle Up, Every Time:** This non-negotiable safety measure protects you in case of an accident. Make sure all passengers in your car are buckled up too.

- **Adjust Your Seat and Mirrors:** A properly adjusted seat and mirrors ensure optimal visibility and control of the vehicle.

- **Minimize Distractions:** Put your phone away! Distracted driving is a leading cause of accidents. Focus on the road, avoid loud music, and limit conversations with passengers.

- **Maintain a Safe Following Distance:** This crucial practice allows enough time to react if the car in front of you stops suddenly. The recommended following distance is typically three to four seconds.

- **Be Predictable:** Signal well in advance before turning or changing lanes. Erratic maneuvers can confuse other drivers and lead to accidents.

- **Night Vision Matters:** Headlights should be turned on at dusk and during low-visibility conditions. Be extra cautious and adjust your speed at night when visibility is reduced. Most cars automatically turn off lights, so there's no reason to not have them on all the time – they help even in daylight.

- **Know Your Limits:** Don't drive when you're tired, drowsy, under the influence of alcohol or drugs, or experiencing any physical limitations that could impair your driving ability.

- **Inspect Your Vehicle Regularly:** Perform basic checks like tire pressure, fluid levels, and proper functioning of lights and signals. Get regular maintenance check-ups by a qualified mechanic.

Self-Advocacy on the Road:

- **Uncomfortable with a Friend's Driving? Speak Up!** If your friend speeds, disregards traffic rules, or drives recklessly, don't be afraid to express your concerns. Offer to switch places or suggest finding another way to travel if they refuse to be a responsible driver.

- **Pulled Over? Stay Calm and Respectful:** Maintain composure, turn on your hazard lights, and pull over to a safe location. Keep your hands visible on the steering wheel and wait for the officer's instructions. If unsure about a request, politely ask for clarification. You have the right to remain silent and request a lawyer if necessary.

- **Mechanic Misdiagnosis? Don't Be Afraid to Ask Questions:** If you suspect a mechanic is recommending unnecessary repairs, don't hesitate to ask for explanations and second opinions. Research common repair costs for your car model beforehand to gain some knowledge before visiting a mechanic.

- **Car Trouble on the Road?** If your car breaks down, pull over to a safe location away from traffic. Turn on your hazard lights and call roadside assistance if available. If you need to exit the car, ensure it's safe to do so and stand away from traffic while waiting for help.

- **Unfamiliar Territory? Ask for Directions!** Getting lost happens! Don't be afraid to ask for directions from a gas station attendant, use your phone's GPS navigation app (safely!), or pull over to a safe location to consult a map.

Advanced Scenarios:

- **Bad Weather Driving:** Adjust your speed significantly during rain, snow, fog, or icy conditions. Increase following distance and allow extra time for travel. Use headlights even during daytime when visibility is poor.

- Sharing the Road with Others: Be aware of motorcycles, bicycles, and pedestrians who may be less visible. Give them ample space and avoid aggressive maneuvers.

- Parallel Parking Woes? Practice Makes Perfect! Find an empty parking lot and practice parallel parking until you feel confident. Utilize online tutorials or ask a licensed driver for guidance.

- Dealing with Aggressive Drivers: Don't engage with road rage! Maintain your lane, avoid eye contact, and don't respond to gestures or honking. If you feel truly threatened, pull over to a safe location when possible and call the police.

Carjackings and Stranger Danger

While statistically rare, carjackings can happen. Here's how to stay vigilant and prioritize your safety:

- Be Aware of Your Surroundings: Avoid stopping in isolated areas, especially at night. Park in well-lit, populated areas whenever possible.

- Lock Your Doors While Driving: Don't leave your car unlocked at intersections or stop signs, even for a brief moment.

- Trust Your Gut: If a situation feels unsafe, it probably is. Don't roll down your windows for strangers, and be prepared to drive away if necessary.

- Have a Plan: Discuss carjacking prevention strategies with your family. Know emergency numbers and consider carrying a personal safety alarm for an extra layer of protection.

- If Confronted: Stay calm and assess the situation. If the carjacker seems calm, consider complying with their demands to minimize the risk of violence. Remember, your life and safety are more important than material possessions.

- Report the Incident: If you are the victim of a carjacking, immediately contact the police and provide a detailed description of the perpetrator and the vehicle.

Teen Passengers: Advocating for Yourself

As a passenger, you also have a right to feel safe. Here's how to speak up:

- **Uncomfortable with the Driver's Behavior?** If the driver is speeding, breaking traffic laws, or driving under the influence, politely express your concerns. Offer to call a taxi or rideshare service if they refuse to drive safely.

- **Seatbelt Safety:** Don't be afraid to ask the driver to pull over if they haven't buckled up. Remind other passengers of the importance of seatbelt use as well.

- **Distracted Driving:** If the driver is texting, talking on the phone, or otherwise distracted, politely request them to put away their phone and focus on the road.

- **Feeling Unsafe?** If a situation feels dangerous, ask the driver to pull over in a safe location. If they refuse, consider calling a trusted adult or emergency services if necessary.

Remember: Your safety is paramount. Don't be afraid to speak up and advocate for yourself, whether you're the driver or a passenger.

Additional Resources:

- National Highway Traffic Safety Administration (NHTSA): https://www.nhtsa.gov/

- The Governors Highway Safety Association (GHSA): https://www.ghsa.org/

- The National Institute for Teen Driving Safety: https://teendriversource.research.chop.edu/

By following these tips and staying vigilant, you can navigate the roads with confidence and ensure a safe and enjoyable driving experience.

Staying Calm and Collected: Traffic Stop Safety and Self-Advocacy for Teens

Getting pulled over can be a nerve-wracking experience, especially for new drivers. This guide equips you with the knowledge and confidence to navigate a traffic stop safely and advocate for yourself respectfully.

Preparation is Key:

- **Know Your Rights:** Familiarize yourself with your state's traffic laws and your rights during a police stop. Understand the documentation you are legally required to present (usually driver's license, registration, and proof of insurance).

- **Practice Makes Perfect:** Talk to your parents or experienced drivers about what to expect during a traffic stop. Practice maintaining composure and speaking politely.

When the Lights Flash:

- **Stay Calm: Don't panic!** Put on your hazard lights, signal your intent to pull over, and find a safe location on the side of the road to stop. Avoid making sudden stops or erratic maneuvers.

- **Turn Off the Engine and Roll Down the Window (Partially):** Turn off the car engine and put the vehicle in park. Roll down your driver's side window partially, but keep the other windows and doors closed unless instructed otherwise.

- **Keep Your Hands Visible:** Place your hands on the steering wheel where the officer can see them. Avoid reaching for your phone, wallet, or glove compartment unless specifically requested.

- **Courtesy is Key:** Be polite and respectful towards the officer. Address them as "officer" or "sir/ma'am." Most officers just want people to be safe.

Documentation and Communication:

- **Wait for Instructions:** The officer will approach your vehicle and explain the reason for the stop. Wait for their instructions before speaking or retrieving any documentation.

- **Provide Requested Documents:** When asked for your license, registration, and proof of insurance, tell the officer where they are, then calmly reach for them (usually in the glove compartment or center console) and hand them to the officer one at a time.

- **Be Honest and Concise:** If you are unsure about something, politely ask for clarification. Answer the officer's questions honestly and to the point. Avoid elaborate explanations or unnecessary details.

What if I Disagree with the Ticket?

- **Respectful Disagreement:** If you believe the ticket was issued in error, you can politely express your disagreement. However, avoid arguing or getting confrontational.

- **Your Options:** Ask the officer to explain the violation further. You may choose to accept the ticket and contest it later in court, or you might be able to resolve the issue on the spot with a warning.

- **Don't Sign Away Your Rights:** Don't sign the ticket unless you understand the charges and intend to pay the fine. Signing the ticket typically signifies you admit guilt, although it doesn't necessarily prevent you from contesting it later.

Additional Scenarios:

- **Search of the Vehicle**: Officers may request to search your car. You have the right to refuse a search (unless they have probable cause). Politely but firmly decline a search if you're uncomfortable with it. You can ask if they have a warrant if you're unsure.

- **Feeling Uncomfortable:** If you feel unsafe or the officer's behavior seems overly aggressive, politely state that you'd like to have a parent or lawyer present.

What NOT to Do:

- **Don't Panic:** Staying calm and collected ensures a smoother interaction with the officer.

- **Don't Admit Fault Unless You're Guilty:** Avoid saying things like "I guess I was speeding" if you're unsure about the violation.

- **Don't Argue or Make Excuses:** Being argumentative or defensive will only escalate the situation.

- **Don't Consent to a Search Without Probable Cause:** You have the right to refuse unreasonable searches.

- **Don't Get Out of the Vehicle Without Instruction:** Stay in your car unless the officer asks you to step out.

What Happens Next?

- **Following Up:** After receiving a ticket, review it carefully. If you decide to contest the ticket, contact your parents, lawyer, or local court for further guidance.

Remember:

- **Knowledge is Power:** Knowing your rights and practicing proper protocol empowers you to handle a traffic stop calmly and confidently.

- **Safety First:** Your safety is the top priority. Be respectful but don't hesitate to advocate for yourself if you feel unsafe.

- **Document Everything:** If you feel the stop wasn't conducted fairly, keep detailed notes of the date, time, location, and the officer's name and badge number.

By following these tips and staying calm, you can navigate a traffic stop effectively and ensure a safe scenario for everyone.

In the Aftermath: Car Crash Safety and Self-Advocacy for Teens

Car accidents can be frightening and confusing, especially for young drivers. This guide equips you with the knowledge and steps to prioritize your safety, assess the situation calmly, and advocate for yourself in the aftermath of a car crash.

Safety First:

- **Check Yourself and Others:** Once the car comes to a complete stop, take a moment to assess yourself for injuries. If possible, check on any passengers in your car. If anyone is seriously injured, call 911 immediately.

- **Turn Off Your Engine and Activate Hazard Lights:** Turning off your engine prevents further hazards and activating your hazard lights alerts oncoming traffic of the accident.

- **Move to Safety (If Possible):** If your car is in a dangerous location (e.g., blocking traffic or on the side of a busy highway), carefully assess if it's safe to exit the vehicle and move to a safe distance from the wreckage. If you cannot move safely, stay in your car with your seatbelt buckled until help arrives.

- **Secure the Scene:** If possible, set out flares or reflective triangles (if you have them) to further alert oncoming traffic to the accident.

Assess the Situation:

- **Gather Information:** If everyone involved seems okay, exchange contact information with the other driver(s) involved in the accident. Get their name, driver's license number, insurance company details, and phone number.

Jennifer Tillock M.S. CCC-SLP

- **Take Pictures (If Possible):** Document the scene of the accident with photos on your phone (if safe to do so). Capture damage to all vehicles involved, skid marks on the road, and any relevant traffic signs or signals. These photos can be helpful evidence later.

- **Write down or make a voice note** of your version of events. It can be hard to remember details even minutes after the accident, and answering questions can muddy your memory.

- **Do Not Admit Fault:** Avoid making statements that could be construed as admitting fault for the accident. Simply explain what happened from your perspective without accepting blame.

Contacting Authorities:

- **Call 911 (If Necessary):** Even if injuries seem minor, it's always best to err on the side of caution and call 911 for medical attention. The police will also need to file an accident report.

- **Cooperate with Law Enforcement:** Answer the officer's questions honestly and to the point. Provide your driver's license, registration, and proof of insurance when requested.

- **Be Respectful:** The aftermath of an accident can be stressful for everyone involved. Maintain composure and be respectful toward officers and other parties.

Self-Advocacy and Next Steps:

- **Don't Discuss the Accident with Third Parties:** Avoid discussing the details of the accident with anyone besides the police, your lawyer, or your insurance company.

- **Seek Medical Attention:** Even if you initially feel okay, get checked out by a doctor to rule out any potential injuries.

- **Contact Your Insurance Company:** Report the accident to your insurance company as soon as possible. They will guide you through the claims process.

- **Gather Additional Witness Information:** If there were any witnesses to the accident, try to obtain their contact information if possible. Their statements can be valuable later.

- **Document Everything:** Keep detailed notes of the accident, including the date, time, location, names of all involved parties, police report details, and any medical reports or repair estimates.

- **Seek Legal Advice (If Necessary):** If dealing with extensive car damage, injuries, or complex insurance disputes, consider consulting with an attorney specializing in car accident cases.

Additional Scenarios:

- **Hit-and-Run:** If you are involved in a hit-and-run accident, immediately call 911 and provide the police with any details you can remember about the other vehicle, such as make, model, and license plate number (if possible).

- **Unfamiliar Territory:** If the accident occurs in an unfamiliar area, wait for emergency services to arrive and guide you. Don't attempt to navigate further if you're unsure of the roads.

- **Disagreements Over Fault:** If there's a disagreement over who caused the accident, don't argue at the scene. Exchange information and let the insurance companies and potentially the police determine fault.

Remember:

- **Safety First:** Your health and well-being are the top priority. Assess the situation calmly and ensure everyone involved is safe before addressing other matters.

- **Be Prepared:** Having a car emergency kit with basic first aid supplies, flares, and a phone charger can be helpful in the event of an accident.

- **Stay Calm and Composed:** Accidents can be confusing and stressful. Focus on clear communication and prioritize factual information rather than emotions when dealing with authorities and insurance companies.

- **Don't Sign Anything Without Review:** Don't be pressured to sign any documents from the other driver's insurance company without thoroughly reviewing them first. Consult with an attorney if unsure about any legal documents.

- **Beware of Scams:** Unfortunately, car accidents can attract fraudulent activity. Be cautious of unsolicited calls or visits from repair shops or medical providers.

Emotional and Legal Support:

- **Talk to Someone:** Car accidents can be emotionally taxing. Talk to a trusted friend, family member, or therapist about your experience.

- **Don't Rush Back on the Road:** If the accident has shaken your confidence behind the wheel, don't feel pressured to drive again immediately. Practice in a controlled environment and seek additional driving lessons if needed.

- **Legal Representation:** If facing legal complications due to the accident, consulting with a qualified car accident lawyer is crucial. They can advise you on your legal rights and navigate the legal process effectively.

Jennifer Tillock M.S. CCC-SLP

Preventing Future Accidents:

- **Stay Focused on the Road:** Avoid distractions like texting, eating, or loud music while driving.

- **Maintain a Safe Following Distance:** Leave ample space between your car and the vehicle in front of you to react in case of sudden stops.

- **Drive According to Weather Conditions:** Adjust your speed and driving style for rain, snow, fog, or icy roads.

- **Never Drive Under the Influence:** Alcohol and drugs significantly impair your driving ability. Always designate a sober driver or use a rideshare service if you've consumed any substances.

- **Regular Car Maintenance:** Regularly maintain your vehicle to ensure it's in safe operating condition.

By prioritizing safety, staying calm in the aftermath, and advocating for yourself effectively, you can navigate a car accident experience with greater confidence and minimize the negative impact on your life.

Scenarios

Loud music bumps as your friend swerves slightly on the drive. An uneasy feeling grows – they're unusually quiet, eyes wide, and a strange smell fills the car. Ready to ditch the party and get home safe.

You get in your friend's car to go to the movies. You notice they seem to be driving faster than you're comfortable with, weaving through traffic and taking corners a little too sharply. Your stomach clenches with anxiety.

You get in your friend's car and notice they didn't buckle up as they pull out of the driveway. They glance over at you and shrug when they see you looking at the empty seatbelt buckle. You're feeling awkward but concerned about your safety.

You're cruising with your friends, laughing and enjoying the ride. Suddenly, they erupt into a playful shoving match, bumping into you in the front seat and momentarily grabbing the steering wheel. You are startled and struggling to maintain control of the car.

You and your friends planned a fun night out, but the weather forecast has taken a turn for the worse, predicting freezing rain and icy roads. Everyone seems excited to go, but you're worried about the hazardous driving conditions.

You pile into your friend's car, ready to head out for the day. As you reach for your seatbelt, you discover it's tangled or stuck and won't buckle properly. Hesitant to speak up and delay the trip, you weigh your options.

You're cruising down the highway with the music pumping when a dog darts out from behind a stopped car. You slam on the brakes instinctively, but a collision seems imminent. In a split second, you consider swerving to avoid the dog, but you're unsure if that would be safer or put yourself and others at risk.

You're behind the wheel, focused on the road, when a wave of dizziness washes over you. The world seems to tilt, and your vision blurs momentarily. You are scared and unsure if it's a passing wave or something more serious.

You're chauffeuring your friends around town, trying to concentrate on the road, but their constant loud talking and boisterous behavior make it difficult. They're yelling over the music, singing along off-key, and generally creating a distracting environment.

You're running late for your shift and stuck in bumper-to-bumper traffic due to a reported accident. Panic starts to rise as the clock ticks closer to your start time. You consider risky options like weaving through traffic or running a red light, but you know the dangers involved.

Leaving the grocery store, you carefully back out of your parking space but accidentally bump the car behind you. There's a minor dent on their bumper, and you can't find the owner anywhere.

Jennifer Tillock M.S. CCC-SLP

It's late after a long study session at the library, and you finally head to your car, exhausted. Your eyelids feel heavy, and you struggle to stay focused on the road. Realizing you're too tired to drive safely, you consider your options.

You're cruising down the road with the windows down when you hear a loud thump and feel a sudden lurch. Pulling over to the side of the road, you discover a flat tire.

You're a new driver, feeling nervous behind the wheel. Suddenly, you see flashing lights in your rearview mirror. Your heart races as you pull over, unsure of the protocol and worried about making a mistake during the interaction with the police officer.

You're driving with a friend, and they accidentally roll down the window to toss out a discarded candy wrapper. Moments later, you see flashing lights behind you. You worry the officer might mistake the litter for something more serious and contemplate how to explain the situation honestly while advocating for your friend.

You're driving home from school when you get pulled over for a broken taillight you weren't aware of. Feeling flustered, you fumble for your registration and license, worried about appearing unprepared or disrespectful to the officer.

You're a passenger in your friend's car when you get pulled over for a minor traffic violation. Your friend starts getting defensive and arguing with the officer, making you feel increasingly tense and unsafe. You grapple with how to advocate for a calmer approach without escalating the situation.

You're driving with an expired license you completely forgot to renew. Shame washes over you as you pull over, worried about the consequences and how to explain your lapse in responsibility to the officer.

You're a passenger in your friend's car when the officer approaches and asks if anyone has been drinking alcohol. Your friend, who had a beer earlier, hesitates and glances at you nervously. Torn between loyalty and honesty, you contemplate how to navigate this tricky situation.

You get pulled over for speeding, but you genuinely believe you were within the limit. Feeling confident but respectful, you wonder how to politely express your disagreement with the officer and inquire about radar verification.

The officer asks you to step out of the vehicle for a routine check. Uncertain if this is standard procedure or something more serious, you question the request politely and inquire about the reason behind it.

You're driving with borrowed license plates on your car while waiting for your permanent ones to arrive. The officer seems suspicious about the temporary plates, and you worry they might not be familiar with the process. You contemplate how to explain the situation clearly and provide any necessary documentation.

You witness the officer's behavior becoming overly aggressive or disrespectful during the interaction. Unsure of your rights and hesitant to escalate the situation, you wonder if there's a safe way to express your concerns about the officer's conduct.

You're pulled over at night while driving home from work. Feeling a surge of fear and vulnerability, you contemplate how to stay calm and ensure your safety during the interaction, especially considering the time and potential isolation.

You're a passenger in a car with friends when the officer asks to search the vehicle. No one has anything illegal, but you're unsure if you have the right to refuse a search or how to politely express your discomfort with the request.

You get pulled over for a minor traffic violation, but you suspect the officer might be racially profiling you or someone else in the car. Feeling frustrated and targeted, you wonder how to address your concerns about potential bias without appearing confrontational.

You're driving with a permit, and the officer notices you're alone in the car without a licensed driver present. Flustered and worried about the legal implications, you contemplate how to explain the situation and inquire about the proper protocol for driving with a learner's permit.

You get pulled over for speeding, but you were rushing someone to the hospital for a medical emergency. Stressed and worried about the person's well-being, you wonder how to explain the urgency of the situation to the officer in a way that garners understanding and leniency.

The officer asks you to take a breathalyzer test, even though you haven't been drinking any alcohol. Unsure of your rights and potential consequences of refusing, you contemplate how to politely request more information about the test and the option to decline.

You're pulled over in an unfamiliar area and don't have your phone readily available for GPS navigation. Feeling lost and unsure how to proceed after receiving a warning, you contemplate how to politely ask the officer for directions to get back on track.

You witness the officer writing you a ticket for a violation you believe is unfair or inaccurate. Feeling frustrated but respectful, you wonder how to inquire about contesting the ticket and the process involved.

The officer asks for your phone to check your social media activity or search for recent messages. Feeling a strong sense of privacy violation, you contemplate how to politely but firmly refuse the request and explain your boundaries.

You're pulled over for a minor traffic violation, but you have a large sum of cash in the car for a legitimate reason (like making a down payment). Nervous about potential suspicion, you consider how to disclose the money to the officer transparently and avoid misunderstandings.

You see flashing lights in your rearview mirror and your heart starts racing. You know you should pull over, but you're unsure if you should grab your registration and license first or wait for the officer to ask for them. Fumbling in your glove compartment while stopped could appear suspicious, but reaching for them before the officer approaches might seem overly anxious.

You're cruising down the highway when you see blue lights flashing behind you. Panic sets in as you realize you're approaching a busy intersection or a narrow bridge with no shoulder. You know you need to pull over, but finding a safe and legal spot feels impossible in the moment.

You're driving through an unfamiliar area, late at night, when you see flashing lights behind you. Fear washes over you as you recognize the blue glow, but you're in a deserted part of town with limited streetlights and no apparent safe haven nearby.

You're driving home from a movie when you see flashing lights in your mirror. However, something seems off - the lights appear a different color or configuration than what you're accustomed to seeing from police vehicles. Unsure if it's a legitimate police car or a potential impersonator, you contemplate how to proceed cautiously and avoid putting yourself in a dangerous situation.

You're a passenger in a car with friends when the driver loses control on a wet road and skids off the highway. Dazed and disoriented, you check yourself for injuries but notice your friend in the backseat seems unresponsive.

You're driving home from school when another car runs a red light and t-bones your vehicle. The impact is strong, the airbags deploy, and you're shaken but seemingly unharmed. However, you notice smoke rising from the engine compartment, raising concerns about a potential fire hazard.

You're stopped at a red light when you get rear-ended by another car. The impact jolts you forward, and you experience a sharp pain in your neck. Adrenaline surges through you, but you're unsure if you should get out of the car or wait for the other driver to approach.

You're driving on a rural road late at night when you hit a deer that suddenly darts into your path. The car sustains some damage, and the deer lies motionless on the side of the road. You aren't sure if the animal is still alive and potentially dangerous.

You're a passenger in a car with your friends when you get caught in a hailstorm. The large hailstones cause the driver to lose visibility, and the car skids off the road into a ditch. Everyone seems okay, but you're stranded in a remote area with limited cell service.

You're driving on a busy freeway when a tire suddenly blows out. The car swerves violently, but you manage to regain control and pull over to the shoulder. Shaken and unsure how to proceed, you contemplate how to change the tire yourself (if you know-how) or call for roadside assistance while staying a safe distance from passing traffic.

You're driving with a friend when you witness a car accident ahead on the road. People seem injured, and debris litters the scene. The urge to help is strong, but you're unsure if it's safe to approach the accident site or if you should prioritize calling emergency services from a safe distance.

You're driving home after a party when you experience a wave of dizziness and lose consciousness momentarily. You regain awareness moments later, thankfully on the shoulder of the road, but you're unsure if you can continue driving safely.

You're a passenger in a car with your friend when they argue with another driver on the road. The situation escalates, and the other driver exits their vehicle in a threatening manner. Frightened for your safety, you contemplate how to de-escalate the situation and convince your friend to drive away from the potential confrontation.

You're driving on a deserted road late at night when you see a car pulled over on the side with its hazard lights flashing. A sense of caution washes over you, and you debate if it's safe to stop and offer assistance or if you should continue driving and report the stranded vehicle to the authorities.

You're cruising down the highway during a snowstorm, but your windshield wipers struggle to keep up with the heavy snowfall. Visibility becomes increasingly limited as ice accumulates on the wiper blades.

You're about to head out for errands when you notice a concerning bulge developing on one of your tires. Upon closer inspection, you see the tread starting to separate from the body of the tire.

It's dusk, that in-between time where the sun has dipped below the horizon but the sky hasn't quite transitioned to darkness. You're unsure if you should turn on your headlights yet, worried about appearing overly cautious, but also concerned about your visibility to other drivers.

You're cruising down a two-lane highway at night when the headlights of an oncoming car seem unusually bright. The glare momentarily blinds you, making it difficult to see the road ahead. You are feeling startled and unsure how to react

You're cruising down the highway at highway speeds when you experience a sudden and alarming vibration in the steering wheel. The car pulls slightly to one side, and the jerking motion intensifies. You are panicked and unsure of the cause.

You're driving down a familiar road at night when you notice oncoming traffic repeatedly flashing their high beams at you. You are confused and unsure why they're signaling you.

You're stopped at a red light in a rough part of town when a stranger approaches your car. They gesture for you to roll down the window, but your gut instinct screams danger.

You're stopped at a red light late at night in a deserted area. Suddenly, you feel a jolt from behind as the car following you bumps your bumper. Noticing the other driver seems agitated, you worry about escalating the situation.

You're driving through a neighborhood known for higher crime rates when your check engine light illuminates on the dashboard. You are unsure of the severity of the problem and concerned about potential car trouble in a potentially unsafe location.

You're cruising down the highway in bumper-to-bumper traffic when your check engine light flickers on. You are stuck in a sea of cars with limited maneuverability.

Online/Social Media

Navigating the Digital Age: Safety and Self-Advocacy for Teens Online

The internet and social media have revolutionized the way we connect, learn, and express ourselves. While these platforms offer endless possibilities, it's crucial for teens to navigate them with a healthy dose of caution and self-awareness. This guide equips you with the knowledge and tools to prioritize your safety, advocate for yourself, and navigate the digital landscape with confidence.

Safety First:

- **Think Before You Click:** Not everything online is what it seems. Be wary of flashy headlines, unsolicited links, or offers that seem too good to be true. Hover over links before clicking to see the actual destination URL.

- **Guard Your Personal Information:** Avoid sharing your address, phone number, or full name with strangers online. Be selective about the information you include on social media profiles.

- **Beware of Phishing Scams:** Phishing emails or messages often mimic legitimate companies or services to trick you into revealing personal information or login credentials. Don't click on suspicious links or attachments.

Building Strong Passwords:

- **Use a Combination of Characters:** Create passwords with a mix of uppercase and lowercase letters, numbers, and symbols. Avoid using dictionary words, birthdays, or easily guessable information.

- **Make Them Unique:** Avoid using the same password for multiple accounts. If remembering complex passwords is difficult, consider using a password manager.

- **Enable Two-Factor Authentication:** Many online platforms offer two-factor authentication, adding an extra layer of security by requiring a code sent to your phone upon login attempts.

Social Media Smarts

- **Privacy Settings:** Review and adjust your privacy settings on all social media platforms. Limit who can see your posts, friend requests, and personal information.

- **Digital Footprint:** Everything you post online leaves a digital footprint. Be mindful of what you share, as it can potentially impact your future education, employment, or even college applications.

- **Beware of Oversharing:** Avoid sharing sensitive information like your location when you check in, upcoming travel plans, or details about your personal life that could be used against you.

Cyberbullying and Online Harassment:

- **Recognize the Signs:** Cyberbullying can include hurtful messages, rumors, exclusion, or threats sent electronically. If you experience this, don't respond directly. Save the evidence (screenshots, messages) and report it to the platform and a trusted adult.

- **Stand Up for Others:** If you witness someone being cyberbullied, offer support to the target and report the abuse. Bystander intervention can make a significant difference.

- **Block and Ignore:** Block bullies from contacting you further and avoid engaging with them. Responding can escalate the situation.

Healthy Online Habits:

- **Balance is Key:** Set healthy boundaries for your social media usage. Schedule breaks throughout the day to disconnect and engage in real-world activities.

- **Critical Thinking:** Don't blindly accept everything you see online. Develop your critical thinking skills to evaluate the credibility of sources and information.

- **Be Mindful of Body Image:** Social media often showcases unrealistic portrayals of beauty and lifestyle. Focus on what makes you unique, and seek inspiration from positive and empowering online communities.

Self-Advocacy in the Digital Age:

- **Know Your Rights:** Familiarize yourself with online privacy laws and your rights regarding your personal information.

- **Report Inappropriate Content:** Most platforms offer options to report harassment, hate speech, or other forms of offensive content. Don't hesitate to use them.

- **Be Assertive:** Have the confidence to politely decline friend requests or messages from strangers who make you uncomfortable.

Building a Positive Online Presence:

- **Share Responsibly:** Be mindful of the content you share online. Avoid posting anything that could be considered offensive or embarrassing to yourself or others.

- **Promote Positive Values:** Use your online voice to support causes you care about and spread positivity through creative content or inspiring messages.

- **Engage Respectfully:** When participating in online discussions, express your views respectfully. Avoid personal attacks and engage in constructive dialogue.

Beyond Safety

- **Digital Citizenship:** Being a responsible digital citizen means using technology ethically and responsibly. This includes respecting intellectual property rights and avoiding plagiarism.

- **Spotting Disinformation:** Misinformation and "fake news" are prevalent online. Develop your skills to identify unreliable sources and verify information before sharing it.

- **Protecting Your Mental Health:** Social media can negatively impact your mental health if you constantly compare yourself to others or engage in negativity. Prioritize activities that promote well-being and online communities that uplift.

Taking Control: Tools and Resources for Teens

Empowering Yourself Online:

- **Privacy Management Tools:** Many social media platforms offer tools to manage your privacy settings and control who sees your content. Explore these features and personalize your settings to maximize control over your online presence.

- **Parental Supervision (With Open Communication):** While maintaining independence is important, open communication with a trusted adult about your online activity can be beneficial. Discuss responsible online behavior and seek guidance when needed. Many parents are happy to learn alongside their teens about navigating the digital world.

- **Reporting Mechanisms:** Most social media platforms have clear reporting mechanisms for cyberbullying, harassment, or inappropriate content. Familiarize yourself with these tools and don't hesitate to use them if you encounter negativity online.

Building a Positive Online Community:

- **Find Your Tribe:** Seek out online communities that share your interests, hobbies, or passions. These platforms can be a source of support, inspiration, and connection with like-minded individuals.

- **Engage with Positive Influencers:** Follow online figures who promote positivity, self-acceptance, and values you resonate with. Their content can uplift and inspire you on your digital journey.

- **Contribute Positively:** Use your online presence to spread kindness, support positive causes, and share your talents or creativity.

Learning Resources:

- **Online Safety Organizations:** Numerous reputable organizations provide resources and educational materials on online safety and responsible digital citizenship. Explore websites of organizations like ConnectSafely, the National Cyber Security Alliance, or the Cyberbullying Research Center.

- **Digital Literacy Courses:** Many schools or libraries now offer digital literacy courses that equip teens with the knowledge and skills to navigate the online world safely and effectively. Consider enrolling in such courses if available.

- **Tech-Savvy Friends and Family:** Connect with friends or family members who are well-versed in technology and can offer advice on online safety practices and responsible social media usage.

The Bottom Line:

The internet and social media can be powerful tools for communication, learning, and self-expression. By prioritizing safety, practicing self-advocacy, and developing digital literacy skills, teens can navigate these platforms confidently and create a positive online presence. Remember, it's your digital world – take control and make the most of it!

Scenarios

You witness a classmate being cyberbullied on social media through a barrage of hurtful messages and comments. You know this behavior is wrong, but you worry about the potential consequences of intervening and becoming a target yourself.

You're scrolling through social media and see a celebrity endorsing a new weight loss tea. Testimonials claim it melts fat away effortlessly. Skeptical of the claims but curious about the product, you wonder how to separate fact from fiction and find reliable information about weight loss.

A notification pops up on your phone - a friend request on social media. The profile picture is generic, and you don't recognize the name. Their message is flattering, but they ask for your phone number to "chat better." A pit forms in your stomach - something feels off about this request.

Witnessing someone viciously target another student with online rumors leaves you conflicted. The victim seems unaware, and you grapple with whether to intervene or stay silent.

You're struggling to log in to your school account at a local coffee shop, the frustration building with each failed attempt. Suddenly, a stranger sitting nearby leans in, claiming they're a tech whiz and can help. Their offer seems helpful, but their close proximity to your screen and intense focus make you uneasy about their motives.

You notice your friend constantly on social media, meticulously crafting a perfect online persona. They seem increasingly withdrawn and fixated on the number of likes and comments they receive. You worry they're attaching their self-worth to online validation.

A social media mishap! You accidentally send a nonsensical message to a stranger's inbox. Their reply seems friendly at first, but quickly takes a turn towards flirting and unwanted familiarity. You feel a knot of unease in your stomach, unsure how to respond without making things worse.

Scrolling social media, a stranger slides into your DMs with a school question. Their follow-up messages get personal fast, making you uneasy but unsure how to respond politely.

You're online shopping and see an amazing deal on a concert ticket, but the website looks a little sketchy. You want to go to the concert, but you're worried the website might be a scam.

You're scrolling through social media when you see a local advertisement for a babysitting job. The pay rate seems too good to be true, and the only contact information is a private message request. Intrigued yet cautious, you consider responding.

You witness your friend being bullied online. Derogatory comments and messages target their appearance or interests. You worry about the emotional impact on your friend and grapple with how to best offer support and encourage them to report the cyberbullying to a trusted adult or online platform.

You receive a text message from an unknown number asking for nude photos in exchange for money. The message is creepy and makes you feel uncomfortable.

You're scrolling through social media and see a friend post something negative about you. The post hurts your feelings, and you're not sure how to react.

A notification buzzes on your phone, revealing a text from an unknown number. The message starts with a generic compliment, but quickly escalates to personal questions. A shiver runs down your spine as you reread the text.

You made a friend online and they ask for your name. You've been chatting with someone on a gaming forum for a few weeks and they seem cool. They casually ask for your real name, hinting at wanting to add you on another platform. You wonder if it's safe to share your full name or if there's a safer alternative.

You made a new friend online and he wants to meet in person. You met someone on social media who shares your love for obscure indie music. They seem interesting, but now they're inviting you to a concert in a city far from yours. Unsure if this is a genuine invitation or a potential safety risk, you contemplate how to respond without being rude.

You made a friend online and they ask where you live. You've been talking to someone online who claims to be your age and live in your state. They seem friendly, but now they're asking for your town or zip code to "see if we're close." This feels like a red flag, and you're unsure how to deflect the question without revealing too much personal information.

You want to sign up for a cool online game but they ask for a credit card number. You found an amazing online game that all your friends are playing. However, signing up requires entering your credit card number. You worry it might be a free trial scam or a website that steals financial information.

You are online with another teenager who has sent you a photo, but no video meetings. You've been chatting with someone online who claims to be your age. They haven't done a video call but sent you a picture of themselves. Now they're pressuring you to meet in person, which makes you uncomfortable since you can't verify their identity.

You settle into a cozy corner of your favorite coffee shop, eager to get some work done. The barista mentions their free Wi-Fi, but when you try to connect, your laptop struggles. A stranger sitting nearby offers to help, whispering their password suggestion over your shoulder. They seem friendly, but the idea of someone knowing your Wi-Fi password makes you uneasy.

You're scrolling through social media when you get a message from someone claiming to be a new student at your school. They haven't appeared on your school social media pages and you haven't seen them around. They seem friendly and mention seeing your profile picture, but you only have selfies and group photos posted, They suggest meeting up at your house to "hang out and get to know each other better."

The phone rings and an enthusiastic voice announces you've won a brand new car! Elated but skeptical, you learn claiming this prize requires giving the caller your name, address, and credit card number over the phone. There's no mention of any contest you entered, and the whole thing sounds too good to be true.

You're scrolling through your favorite social media platform when you see a challenge with a catchy name and seemingly harmless dare. Everyone in your friend group seems to be participating, posting videos of themselves completing the challenge. However, this particular challenge involves trying a new food combination that looks questionable at best, and you worry it might be dangerous or unhealthy.

You excitedly open an email notification from a popular clothing brand you follow. The email advertises a limited-time offer with an unbelievable discount on their latest collection. Tempted by the chance to snag trendy clothes at a fraction of the price, you click the link in the email. However, upon closer inspection, the website URL seems slightly off compared to the brand's official website, and the design appears a little amateurish.

You're happily chatting with a new friend online who shares your passion for coding. They casually mention they found a website offering free access to premium coding software, something that usually costs a hefty subscription fee. Excited about the prospect, you click the link they send, but upon closer look, the website design appears cluttered and the download button seems suspicious.

You receive a friend request on social media from a stranger with a seemingly perfect profile. Their photos showcase exotic vacations and luxurious hobbies, and their follower count is impressive. They send you a flattering message praising your taste in music and asking to be friends. However, something about their profile feels inauthentic.

While browsing online reviews for a new restaurant you're considering, you notice a growing trend of negative comments. Customers complain about poor hygiene, rude staff, and even potential food poisoning incidents. Despite the red flags, your friends are still enthusiastic about trying the restaurant.

You're logged into a public Wi-Fi network at the library, trying to finish an important online assignment. A notification pops up on your screen prompting you to update your social media app. While you usually update your apps regularly, being on a public network makes you nervous about entering your login information.

While scrolling through social media, you stumble upon a heated debate between two groups of influencers you follow. The disagreement centers around a controversial social issue, and the comments are becoming increasingly hostile and vitriolic. You feel strongly about the topic yourself, but you're hesitant to wade into the online argument for fear of being personally attacked or dragged into the negativity.

You excitedly participate in a live stream hosted by your favorite gamer. The streamer announces a giveaway for exclusive in-game items, prompting viewers to donate money and enter their usernames in the chat for a chance to win.

You receive a private message from a classmate complaining about a teacher's grading practices. They encourage you to join them in a group message where other students are venting their frustrations and planning to confront the teacher collectively.

A stranger slides into your DMs on social media, offering to promote your creative content (art, music, writing) to a wider audience. They claim to have a large following and promise to boost your online presence significantly.

You're reading an article online about a hot-button social issue. The comments section is filled with strong opinions and opposing viewpoints. You feel compelled to contribute your own perspective to the discussion, but you're worried about engaging in an online argument with strangers, especially if the conversation turns disrespectful or unproductive.

You come across a clickbait article with a sensational headline promising to reveal shocking secrets about a celebrity you admire. Despite your curiosity, you've been burned by clickbait before, leading to misleading information and frustrating dead-end links.

You're scrolling through your feed when a friend excitedly posts about a new weight loss supplement they're promoting. They rave about the results and even offer a discount code for your purchase. However, you notice it's clearly a sponsored post, and you're unsure if your friend genuinely likes the product or is simply endorsing it for the money.

You constantly see your friends posting seemingly perfect photos on social media, showcasing flawless bodies and extravagant lifestyles. You start comparing yourself and feeling insecure about your own appearance and experiences. You wonder how to navigate social media while maintaining a healthy self-image and avoiding the pressure to portray an unrealistic online persona.

You're researching a school project online and stumble upon conflicting information about a particular topic. Some websites present dramatic claims with biased language, while others offer factual data with a neutral tone. You struggle to discern reliable sources from misleading information and worry about falling victim to "fake news" that reinforces your existing beliefs.

You're having a fun day with friends and capture the moment with a spontaneous group photo. One friend insists on posting the picture on social media, tagging everyone's profiles. However, you're uncomfortable with the idea of the photo being public and worry about potential privacy breaches or negative comments.

While playing an online multiplayer game, you encounter a group of players who become verbally abusive and resort to personal attacks after losing a round. The experience is upsetting and ruins the enjoyment of the game.

You notice a trend on social media where users with high follower counts and "likes" seem to hold more sway and influence. This makes you feel pressured to constantly curate your online presence to gain popularity, even if it means compromising your authenticity or engaging in activities you're not genuinely interested in.

You find yourself constantly checking your social media feeds throughout the day, feeling anxious if you miss notifications or updates. You realize this constant online engagement might be impacting your productivity and real-world interactions.

You notice your social media feed primarily showcasing content and viewpoints that align with your existing beliefs. You wonder if the platform's algorithms are creating "filter bubbles" that limit your exposure to diverse perspectives and potentially hinder critical thinking skills.

You're writing a funny story about a recent experience and plan to share it on social media. However, you hesitate because some details involve inside jokes with a friend, and you're unsure if it's okay to share them publicly without your friend's knowledge or consent.

You receive an email seemingly from a popular online service you use, claiming your account requires immediate verification due to suspicious activity. The email prompts you to click a link and enter your login credentials. You are suspicious of the email's legitimacy.

Working

Stepping Up at Work: Safety and Self-Advocacy for Teens

The teenage years are a time of exploration, independence, and often, your first foray into the world of work. While earning your own money and gaining valuable experience can be exciting, it's crucial to understand the importance of safety and self-advocacy in any work environment.

This guide equips you with the knowledge and tools to navigate your first job confidently, ensuring your well-being and maximizing your positive work experience.

Safety First: Knowing Your Rights

Every workplace has a legal obligation to provide a safe environment for its employees. This includes:

- **Hazard-Free Environments:** Your employer must ensure the work area is free from potential dangers like electrical hazards, unsafe equipment, or hazardous materials.

- **Proper Training:** You have the right to receive training on any tasks you're assigned, including instructions on safe operation of equipment and proper handling of potentially hazardous materials.

- **Personal Protective Equipment (PPE):** If your job requires using specific equipment like gloves, masks, or safety glasses, your employer is responsible for providing it.

What to Do if You Feel Unsafe

If you ever feel unsafe at work, don't hesitate to address the issue:

- **Speak Up:** Inform your supervisor or manager about the specific hazard or unsafe situation.

- **Document Everything:** Write down the details of the incident, including the date, time, and what happened. Keep a record for your own reference and potential future action.

Jennifer Tillock M.S. CCC-SLP

- **Seek Help:** If your supervisor doesn't address the issue, consider reporting it to the local health and safety department. They can investigate and ensure your workplace complies with safety regulations.

Knowing Your Limits: Lifting, Pushing, and Carrying

Teens are still developing physically, meaning there are limitations to what you can safely lift and carry. It's essential to be aware of safe lifting practices:

- **Know Your Limits:** Don't attempt to lift anything that feels heavy or uncomfortable. Ask for help if something seems too big or bulky to handle alone.

- **Proper Technique:** Learn proper lifting techniques, like bending at your knees and keeping your back straight, to avoid injury.

- **Don't Be Afraid to Say No:** You have the right to refuse to lift something you feel is unsafe for you.

The Importance of Breaks and Rest Time

Taking breaks is crucial for maintaining focus, avoiding fatigue, and minimizing potential accidents. Most workplaces have designated breaks and lunch periods. If you're unsure, ask your supervisor or consult the employee handbook.

Self-Advocacy: Making Your Voice Heard

Self-advocacy is about speaking up for yourself and your needs in a respectful and professional manner. Here's how to practice it at work:

- **Communicate Clearly:** If you're unclear about a task or need additional training, don't hesitate to ask for clarification.

- **Work Schedule:** Talk to your supervisor if your work schedule conflicts with your schoolwork, extracurricular activities, or other commitments.

- **Uncomfortable Situations:** If you face harassment, discrimination, or disrespect from coworkers or customers, speak up and report the incident to a manager or supervisor.

Additional Tips for Working Teens:

- **Know Your Rights:** Familiarize yourself with local labor laws and regulations for teen workers, including minimum wage, working hours, and break times.

- **Maintain Open Communication:** Keep an open line of communication with your manager and don't hesitate to ask questions or voice concerns.

- **Document Everything:** Keep a record of your work schedule, training received, and any safety incidents you encounter.

- **Know Your Emergency Exits:** Be aware of the location of all emergency exits and evacuation procedures in your workplace.

- **Work Smart, Not Hard:** Ask seasoned colleagues for tips on how to be efficient and prioritize your tasks thoughtfully.

- **Respect Your Body**: Be mindful of physical limitations and prioritize taking breaks.

Navigating Specific Workplace Challenges:

This section explores common challenges teens might face in various work environments and offers strategies for maintaining safety and self-advocacy.

Retail:

- **Customer Service:** Retail often involves interacting with a diverse range of customers. If you encounter a rude or aggressive customer, remain calm and polite. If the situation escalates, seek help from a supervisor.

- **Cash Handling:** Be aware of proper cash handling procedures to avoid errors or shortages. Don't hesitate to ask for clarification if unsure about handling specific transactions.

- **Long Hours on Your Feet:** Retail work often involves standing for extended periods. Wear comfortable shoes and utilize breaks for stretching or light movement to prevent fatigue.

Food Service:

- **Food Safety:** Foodborne illnesses can spread easily in restaurant kitchens. Follow all food safety protocols, including proper hand-washing techniques and maintaining food storage temperatures.

- **Hot Surfaces and Equipment:** Kitchens are full of hot surfaces and equipment. Wear proper oven mitts and learn safe handling procedures to avoid burns.

- **Heavy Lifting:** Lifting heavy pots, food trays, or supplies is common in restaurants. Utilize proper lifting techniques and don't hesitate to ask for help with bulky items.

Yardwork and Landscaping:

- Power Tools: Always wear proper personal protective equipment (PPE) like goggles, earplugs, and gloves when operating power tools. Never use tools you haven't received training on.

- **Working in All Weather Conditions:** Be prepared for changing weather conditions. Dress appropriately and wear sunscreen on hot days. If the weather becomes severe, don't hesitate to ask to take shelter or pause work.

- **Animal Encounters:** You might encounter animals like wasps, bees, or stray dogs while working outdoors. Be aware of potential hazards and know how to react safely if confronted by an animal.

Movie Theater:

- **Late-Night Shifts:** Movie theaters often have late-night shifts. Be aware of your surroundings and ensure you have a safe way to get home after work, especially if working alone.

- **Loud Noises:** Movie theaters can get loud, especially during action sequences. If you have sensitive hearing, consider using earplugs for short periods to protect your ears.

- **Crowded Environments:** Movie theaters can get crowded, especially during premieres or popular releases. Be aware of your surroundings and ensure emergency exits are clear in case of an evacuation.

Remember:

- **Don't Be Afraid to Ask Questions:** There's no shame in asking questions, especially if you're unsure about a task or safety procedure.

- **Trust Your Gut:** If a situation feels unsafe or uncomfortable, it probably is. Don't hesitate to remove yourself from the situation and report the issue to a supervisor.

- **Know When to Say No:** It's okay to say no to a task you feel unqualified for or unsafe completing. Your health and well-being are paramount.

Empowering Yourself for Success:

Your first job can be a valuable learning experience, equipping you with skills and knowledge that benefit you throughout your career. By prioritizing safety, self-advocacy, and open communication, you'll navigate your work environment with confidence and pave the way for future success.

Jennifer Tillock M.S. CCC-SLP

Scenarios

The parents are running late, and the normally well-behaved 5-year-old you're babysitting is getting restless. They start asking to play outside, but it's getting dark and you haven't discussed outdoor play with the parents. You worry about letting them out unsupervised but also hate to disappoint them.

The family dog is usually friendly, but you've never been left alone with it before. The dog seems excited during playtime with the children, and you're unsure how to handle the situation if it gets overly playful or aggressive.

While putting the kids to bed, you hear a strange noise coming from downstairs. You're unsure if it's something serious or just the house settling, but you're home alone and feeling a little scared.

The parents mentioned a specific bedtime routine for the children, but one child throws a tantrum and refuses to cooperate. You try to implement the routine as instructed, but the child becomes increasingly upset.

You open the door to find a stranger at the doorstep claiming to be a friend of the parents needing to use the phone urgently. However, you weren't told about anyone visiting, and the person seems flustered and impatient.

The parents instructed you to give the baby a bottle every 4 hours, but the baby seems hungry sooner and starts crying hysterically. You're unsure if it's okay to deviate from the schedule or if you should wait for the next feeding time.

The older child you're babysitting asks you to help them with their homework, a subject you're unfamiliar with. You don't want to let them down but also worry about giving them the wrong information.

While playing a game with the children, you accidentally knock over a valuable family heirloom. The kids are scared and you worry about how to break the news to the parents when they return.

The child you're babysitting starts complaining of a stomachache. You check their temperature and it seems a little elevated, but you're unsure if you should call the parents or try home remedies first.

The parents are out much later than expected, leaving you alone with the children for an extended period. You start to feel overwhelmed and wish you'd clarified how long you'd be responsible for them.

You're happily playing a board game with the kids when one of them starts arguing about the rules and refuses to lose. The situation escalates, and you worry about maintaining a fun atmosphere while also teaching them about good sportsmanship.

The younger child you're babysitting keeps wanting to climb on the furniture, despite your repeated warnings. You're concerned about their safety but also hesitant to seem overly strict or controlling.

The parents left a specific amount of money for takeout, but it's not enough to cover the delivery fee. You're unsure if it's okay to use a little extra for the delivery or if you should stick to the exact amount provided.

The child you're watching seems withdrawn and uninterested in playing. You try to engage them in different activities, but they remain quiet and distant. You wonder if something is wrong or if they're simply shy around new people.

The parents neglected to mention any allergies the children might have. While offering snacks, you realize one child seems hesitant about something specific. Unsure if it's an allergy or a personal preference, you worry about accidentally causing a reaction.

The doorbell rings persistently, and you're hesitant to answer it since the parents haven't mentioned anyone else coming by. You feel pressured to answer but also prioritize the safety of the children you're watching.

The power suddenly goes out, plunging the house into darkness. The children become scared, and you scramble to find flashlights and candles while reassuring them and maintaining a sense of calm.

The parents mentioned a bedtime story, but you're not familiar with any children's books in the house. You worry about disappointing the

kids but also don't want to make up a story that might be inappropriate.

The child entrusted to your care starts asking personal questions about your life, including your age, relationship status, and even your address. You feel uncomfortable sharing private information but also don't want to seem rude or dismissive.

The parents forgot to mention the pet needs to be let out for a walk at a specific time. However, you're unfamiliar with the neighborhood and slightly nervous about taking the pet outside alone, especially if it's a larger animal.

The lunch rush is on, and the pressure to take orders and complete tasks quickly is intense. You notice a coworker taking shortcuts with food preparation, potentially compromising food safety guidelines. Do you prioritize speed or speak up about the potential health risks?

A customer becomes irate and verbally abusive because their order is taking longer than expected. You feel disrespected and unsure how to handle the situation professionally while maintaining your composure under pressure.

The manager schedules you for a closing shift you weren't previously aware of, conflicting with a previously committed school activity. You worry about letting down your team but also value your academic commitments. How can you advocate for yourself while remaining a reliable employee?

You overhear a group of coworkers gossiping about another employee, making negative comments about their appearance or work ethic. Feeling uncomfortable with the negativity, you wonder if you should intervene or stay silent.

While cleaning the restroom, you discover a customer left a valuable item behind. You know you should report it to a manager, but you're tempted to keep it for yourself. How can you resist this temptation and prioritize honesty?

The register you're working on malfunctions, displaying incorrect prices or refusing to process payments. You worry about customer frustration and potential accusations of errors on your part. How can you address the situation effectively while minimizing inconvenience?

A coworker asks you to cover a longer shift because they're feeling unwell. While you're willing to help, covering the extra time would make you late for your own evening job. How can you communicate your limitations while still being supportive?

The restaurant is unexpectedly inspected by health officials. You're aware of a minor cleaning oversight in your assigned area. Do you confess to the inspector or hope they miss it, potentially jeopardizing the restaurant's rating?

You witness a manager treating a coworker unfairly, assigning them excessive tasks or making discriminatory remarks. Upset by this behavior, you wonder if you should speak up in defense of your colleague or stay out of it to avoid potential conflict.

You're struggling to keep up with the workload during a busy shift. Feeling overwhelmed and frazzled, you accidentally spill a hot beverage on yourself. Do you prioritize tending to your burn or focus on completing customer orders first?

The lunch rush is on, and the pressure to take orders and complete tasks quickly is intense. You notice a coworker taking shortcuts with food preparation, potentially compromising food safety guidelines. Do you prioritize speed or speak up about the potential health risks?

A customer becomes irate and verbally abusive because their order is taking longer than expected. You feel disrespected and unsure how to handle the situation professionally while maintaining your composure under pressure.

The manager schedules you for a closing shift you weren't previously aware of, conflicting with a previously committed school activity. You worry about letting down your team but also value your academic commitments. How can you advocate for yourself while remaining a reliable employee?

You overhear a group of coworkers gossiping about another employee, making negative comments about their appearance or work ethic. Feeling uncomfortable with the negativity, you wonder if you should intervene or stay silent.

While cleaning the restroom, you discover a customer left a valuable item behind. You know you should report it to a manager, but you're tempted to keep it for yourself. How can you resist this temptation and prioritize honesty?

The register you're working on malfunctions, displaying incorrect prices or refusing to process payments. You worry about customer frustration and potential accusations of errors on your part. How can you address the situation effectively while minimizing inconvenience?

A coworker asks you to cover a longer shift because they're feeling unwell. While you're willing to help, covering the extra time would make you late for your own evening job. How can you communicate your limitations while still being supportive?

The restaurant is unexpectedly inspected by health officials. You're aware of a minor cleaning oversight in your assigned area. Do you confess to the inspector or hope they miss it, potentially jeopardizing the restaurant's rating?

You witness a manager treating a coworker unfairly, assigning them excessive tasks or making discriminatory remarks. Upset by this behavior, you wonder if you should speak up in defense of your colleague or stay out of it to avoid potential conflict.

You're struggling to keep up with the workload during a busy shift. Feeling overwhelmed and frazzled, you accidentally spill a hot beverage on yourself. Do you prioritize tending to your burn or focus on completing customer orders first?

You're tasked with stocking shelves high up on a ladder. Feeling nervous about heights, you question your ability to safely complete the task, especially if the ladder feels unsteady or you can't reach certain items.

A heavy box falls from a higher shelf and narrowly misses you as you're restocking nearby. Shaken and unsure if you were injured, you worry about reporting the incident or brushing it off to avoid seeming dramatic.

You're assigned to clean up a spill in the back storage area, but the cleaning supplies haven't been properly labeled. Unsure of the contents or potential hazards, you hesitate to use them without clarification and worry about accidentally damaging merchandise or harming yourself.

A coworker asks you to help them lift a large box that clearly exceeds the weight limit for a single person. While eager to be helpful, you're concerned about potential back injuries or muscle strain from improper lifting techniques.

The store manager asks you to stay late to complete additional tasks you weren't informed about beforehand. You already have plans after work and worry about disappointing the manager or seeming unreliable by refusing.

You witness a customer shoplifting merchandise and stuffing items into their bag. Torn between confronting the customer or discreetly alerting a manager, you worry about

Jennifer Tillock M.S. CCC-SLP

potential escalation or getting involved in a difficult situation.

A customer approaches you with a question about a specific product, but you're unfamiliar with its features and benefits. Feeling unprepared and unsure of the correct information, you hesitate to answer and potentially mislead the customer.

The store is having a busy sale, and the aisles are packed with customers. You notice a fire exit blocked by overflowing merchandise, potentially creating a safety hazard in case of an emergency. Do you speak up about the issue or assume someone else will address it?

You're working alone in the store late at night when a suspicious person lingers near the entrance. Feeling uneasy and unsure of their intentions, you worry about calling security and potentially overreacting or appearing timid.

You're tasked with operating a heavy machinery piece like a pallet jack or forklift, equipment you haven't received proper training on. Unsure of the controls or potential safety risks, you hesitate to operate the machinery without proper guidance.

The store receives a new shipment with damaged packaging on several boxes. Unsure if the contents are compromised or require further inspection, you question whether to simply stock the items or alert a manager about the potential damage.

You're organizing merchandise on a high shelf when you notice a potentially defective electrical cord powering a nearby display.

Sparks and a burning smell raise concerns, but you hesitate to unplug the cord without authorization or potentially disrupting store operations.

The store manager encourages you to participate in a "friendly competition" with other employees to see who can stock shelves the fastest. While eager to prove yourself, you worry about prioritizing speed over accuracy or potentially compromising safety procedures to win the competition.

A customer approaches you with a damaged or malfunctioning product they purchased earlier. Unsure of the store's return policy or how to handle the situation, you're caught between assisting the customer and needing to involve a manager for further guidance.

You're working the cash register when a customer attempts to use a coupon that seems expired or potentially fraudulent. Feeling pressured to complete the transaction quickly, you struggle with how to verify the coupon's validity without causing a scene at the register.

The store announces a mandatory fire safety training session scheduled for your regular shift. However, you have a pre-existing commitment to a school event you can't reschedule. Unsure of the consequences for missing the training, you worry about balancing your work responsibilities with your academic commitments.

You overhear a group of coworkers gossiping about a customer's appearance or making discriminatory remarks. Feeling uncomfortable with the negativity and potential bias, you wonder if you should report the incident to a manager or avoid getting involved.

While sorting through returned merchandise, you discover a customer left behind a personal item containing sensitive information like credit cards or identification documents. Torn between keeping it safe or discarding it accidentally, you grapple with the responsibility of handling lost and found items.

The store's inventory system malfunctions, displaying inaccurate stock levels for certain items. Customers become frustrated when you inform them of unavailable items listed as "in stock." You struggle to manage customer frustration while dealing with a faulty system.

You're tasked with cleaning a cluttered stockroom with narrow pathways and uneven surfaces. Concerned about potential tripping hazards or falling objects, you question if the workspace is safe for completing your assigned tasks effectively.

The crew leader assigns you a task that involves using power tools like a hedge trimmer or leaf blower. You haven't received proper training on their safe operation and worry about injuring yourself or damaging property if you use them incorrectly.

While trimming a hedge, you accidentally nick a sprinkler head, causing a water leak. Unsure of how to fix the leak or if it's your responsibility to deal with it, you worry about causing further damage or inconveniencing your coworkers.

You're working alongside a more experienced crew member who seems to be cutting corners on safety protocols, neglecting protective gear or taking unnecessary risks while climbing trees.

The weather takes a turn for the worse, with heavy rain or extreme heat suddenly replacing clear skies. The crew leader insists on continuing work, but you worry about the potential health risks or hazards associated with working in these conditions.

You're tasked with lifting and hauling heavy bags of mulch or landscaping materials. Feeling overwhelmed by the weight and unsure of proper lifting techniques, you worry about back injuries or muscle strain if you attempt the task alone.

A client approaches you and expresses dissatisfaction with the work completed so far, criticizing your trimming technique or the placement of plants. Unsure how to handle the criticism professionally or if you should report the issue to the crew leader.

You encounter a group of aggressive animals like wasps or a territorial dog while working on a client's property. Feeling threatened and unsure of how to handle the situation, you worry about getting stung or bitten if you don't react appropriately.

The crew leader asks you to use a pesticide or herbicide you're unfamiliar with. You haven't been informed about the proper application methods or potential safety hazards associated with the chemicals.

You discover a hidden object like old tools, rusty nails, or even potential hazardous waste buried in the client's yard. Unsure of how to handle the situation safely or if you should alert your crew leader to investigate further.

While raking leaves, you accidentally damage a client's outdoor property, like knocking over a decorative statue or scratching a newly painted fence. Feeling responsible and worried about the client's reaction, you grapple with how to best report the incident.

The crew leader instructs everyone to climb a tall ladder to trim a tree branch, but you have a fear of heights and feel shaky on unstable surfaces. Torn between completing the task and expressing your fear, you worry about holding back the team or potentially putting yourself at risk.

You're working in a client's yard with a swimming pool, and a young child wanders unsupervised near the edge. Concerned about the child's safety but unsure if it's your place to intervene, you grapple with how to discreetly alert the homeowner or another adult.

The crew is tasked with clearing overgrown brush or removing debris from a neglected yard. You suspect there might be hidden hazards like broken glass, rusty nails, or even animal nests in the overgrown areas.

While operating a lawnmower, you accidentally hit a hidden sprinkler head or buried cable line, causing damage to the property infrastructure. Unsure if you should report the incident immediately or try to fix the damage yourself, you worry about potential consequences or getting in trouble.

The weather forecast predicts heavy rain later in the day, but the crew leader hasn't provided any rain gear or instructions for working in wet conditions. Feeling unprepared and unsure if it's safe to continue working, you wonder if you should speak up or follow orders.

You're tasked with using a powerful weed wacker for the first time. The loud noise and forceful vibrations make you feel uncomfortable and unsure about handling the tool safely.

While trimming bushes, you encounter a swarm of insects or a beehive hidden within the foliage. Feeling threatened and unsure if you're allergic to stings, you worry about a potential allergic reaction if you don't react quickly.

The crew leader assigns you a task that involves using a gas-powered tool like a leaf blower or edger. You haven't been trained on proper safety protocols like refueling procedures or how to handle potential engine malfunctions.

You're tasked with cleaning up a client's yard after a party, and you discover discarded food scraps or spilled drinks attracting unwanted pests like rodents or raccoons. Worried about potential animal encounters or the spread of disease, you wonder if you should mention it to the crew leader or try to handle it discreetly.

While working in a client's yard, you discover a valuable item like lost jewelry or a forgotten phone hidden among the foliage. Torn between keeping it safe or returning it directly to the homeowner, you wonder about proper protocol for handling lost and found items on the job.

A customer becomes irate and verbally abusive because their preferred seat is unavailable, despite them not purchasing reserved seating. You feel disrespected and unsure how to handle the situation professionally while maintaining a composure in a potentially crowded lobby.

The manager assigns you to clean a spilled beverage in a dark and cluttered storage room. Concerned about tripping hazards or electrical cords, you hesitate to proceed without proper lighting or ensuring the spilled liquid isn't hazardous.

A group of rowdy teenagers enter the theater and seem disruptive, talking loudly and potentially throwing popcorn. Unsure if you should intervene directly or seek help from a supervisor, you worry about escalating the situation or not addressing potential customer disturbances.

The projector malfunctions mid-movie, causing the screen to go blank and the sound to cut out. Unsure of how to troubleshoot the issue or how long it might take to fix, you face frustrated patrons and limited technical knowledge.

A customer approaches you with a medical emergency, like a coughing fit or fainting spell. Uncertain of the severity of the situation and lacking formal first-aid training, you worry about how to respond effectively while waiting for help to arrive.

A fight breaks out between patrons over spilled popcorn or disagreements about seating arrangements. Feeling unsafe and unsure of how to de-escalate the situation, you wonder if you should intervene or alert a supervisor immediately.

You witness a coworker sneaking free food or drinks for themselves or their friends. Torn between ignoring the behavior or reporting it to management, you worry about causing conflict or not upholding company policies.

The theater manager pressures you to stay late to clean up after a particularly busy night, even though you weren't informed of the extended closing time and have pre-existing commitments. You struggle to advocate for your scheduled time off while fulfilling your job responsibilities.

A customer requests to use your phone charger behind the concession stand counter. Unsure of company policy regarding personal item use in restricted areas, you hesitate to allow it but also don't want to seem discourteous.

You're tasked with cleaning a restroom stall with a malfunctioning lock, potentially leaving it unusable for patrons. Unsure if you can mark it out of service or need to find a manager for further assistance, you worry about customer inconvenience and potential safety concerns.

You're working the concession stand during a sold-out show for a highly anticipated movie. The demand is overwhelming, and the pressure to quickly serve a long line of impatient customers can be stressful. You worry about maintaining accuracy and quality service while keeping up with the fast pace.

A customer tries to enter the theater with a large bag or backpack that isn't allowed according to security protocols. Unsure if you have the authority to enforce the policy or if it's best to defer to a security guard, you worry about potential conflict or letting someone in who might pose a security risk.

The theater experiences a power outage during a movie screening, plunging the lobby and auditorium into darkness. Panicked patrons might stumble or become frightened. Unsure of the situation's cause or how long the outage will last, you need to maintain calm and communicate effectively with patrons.

You witness a customer attempting to sneak a prohibited item, like outside food or alcohol, into the theater. Torn between ignoring the behavior or politely confronting them about the policy violation, you worry about escalating the situation or not upholding theater rules.

A patron requests a movie ticket refund because they dislike the film or are unhappy with their seating location. Unsure of the theater's refund policy and hesitant to offer a full refund without manager approval, you struggle to navigate the customer's dissatisfaction while following company guidelines.

While cleaning a theater after a showing, you discover a lost or forgotten item, potentially containing valuables like wallets or electronics. Unsure of the proper protocol for handling lost and found items, you worry about misplaced valuables or potential accusations of theft.

A coworker asks you to cover a longer shift because they're feeling unwell. While you're sympathetic and willing to help, covering the extra time might interfere with your own transportation arrangements or study plans. You need to communicate your limitations while offering support.

The theater manager announces a mandatory cleaning protocol for all restrooms, including procedures for handling potentially hazardous materials like biohazards or bodily fluids. You haven't received proper training on these procedures and feel unprepared for the assigned task.

The theater experiences a sudden influx of patrons, potentially due to a nearby event or a last-minute rush. The concession stand becomes overwhelmed with orders, and you struggle to manage the high volume of customers while maintaining quality service and efficiency.

You overhear a group of coworkers gossiping about a customer's appearance or making discriminatory remarks. Feeling uncomfortable with the negativity and potential bias, you wonder if you should report the incident to a manager or avoid getting involved.

Additional Materials

Rubrics

Basic Rubric

	2 points	1 point	0 points
Steps	Student is able to identify all steps in solution	Student is able to identify at least 50% of steps	Student is able to identify less than 50% of steps
Clarity	Student is able to explain reasoning clearly enough that listener can follow without needing clarification	Student is able to explain reasoning so that the listener can follow with some difficulty – prompting for clarification or details may be necessary	Student is unable to explain reasoning in a clear enough fashion that the listener can follow.
Reasoning	Student is able to give reasoning or justification for each step.	Student can give reasoning for at least 50% of steps.	Student is able to give reasoning for less than 50% of steps.
Correctness	Student is able to arrive at an appropriate solution with the correct sequence of steps.	Student arrives at a solution with only a few mistakes or necessary prompting.	Student is unable to come up with a solution without heavy prompting.

Total _____/8 points

Problem Solving Rubric

	2	1	0
Identifies Problem	The student states the problem.	The student identifies the problem with help.	The student does not identify the problem even with help.
Identifies Solution	The student provides a detailed solution including steps to follow.	The student gives a simple solution or needs help.	The student is unable to give a solution even with help, or the solution does not address the problem.
Identifies multiple solutions	The student provides two acceptable solutions.	The student provides only one solution and needs help to find two solutions.	The student is unable to provide more than one solution.
Reasoning	The student provides a detailed explanation of why their solution would work, including some obstacles necessary to overcome.	The student provides a simple explanation of the solution.	The student is unable to provide reasoning of the solution.
Making Predictions	The student appropriately predicts the outcome of their solution.	The student attempts to predict the outcome but needs help.	The student is unable to provide a prediction even with help.
Practicality	The student's solution would typically work.	The student's solution might work, but it is uncertain or awkward.	The student's solution is impractical or won't work.
Connections	The student is able to reflect on a past situation that was similar.	The student attempts to make a connection but needs help.	The student is not able to make personal connections to the situation.
Effort	The student appears to give the scenario sufficient thought and discussion.	The student attempts thought and discussion with teacher prompts.	The student gives little effort or thought to the scenario and discussion.

Total: _____/16

Self-Advocacy Rubric

	2	1	0
What do you need help with?	Able to clearly state what help is needed.	Able to refer to the help needed but needs prompting to fully explore.	Unable to determine what help is needed even with help.
What do you do?	Several steps included in response.	Simple or one-step answer.	No response.
What do you say?	Responds in 1st person.	Response is in 3rd person or needs prompting.	No repsonse.
Appropriate	Response is appropriate to the situation.	Response might be awkward or unusual.	Response is inappropriate to the situation.
Effective	Response would be effective with minimal assistance or difficulty.	Response requires prompting to be effective.	Response would not work.
Understanding	Response shows good understanding of scenario.	Response shows a minor misunderstanding or prompting needed.	Response is off-topic or shows no understanding of the scenario.

Total: _____/12

Jennifer Tillock M.S. CCC-SLP

Visual Aids

Fishbone Diagram

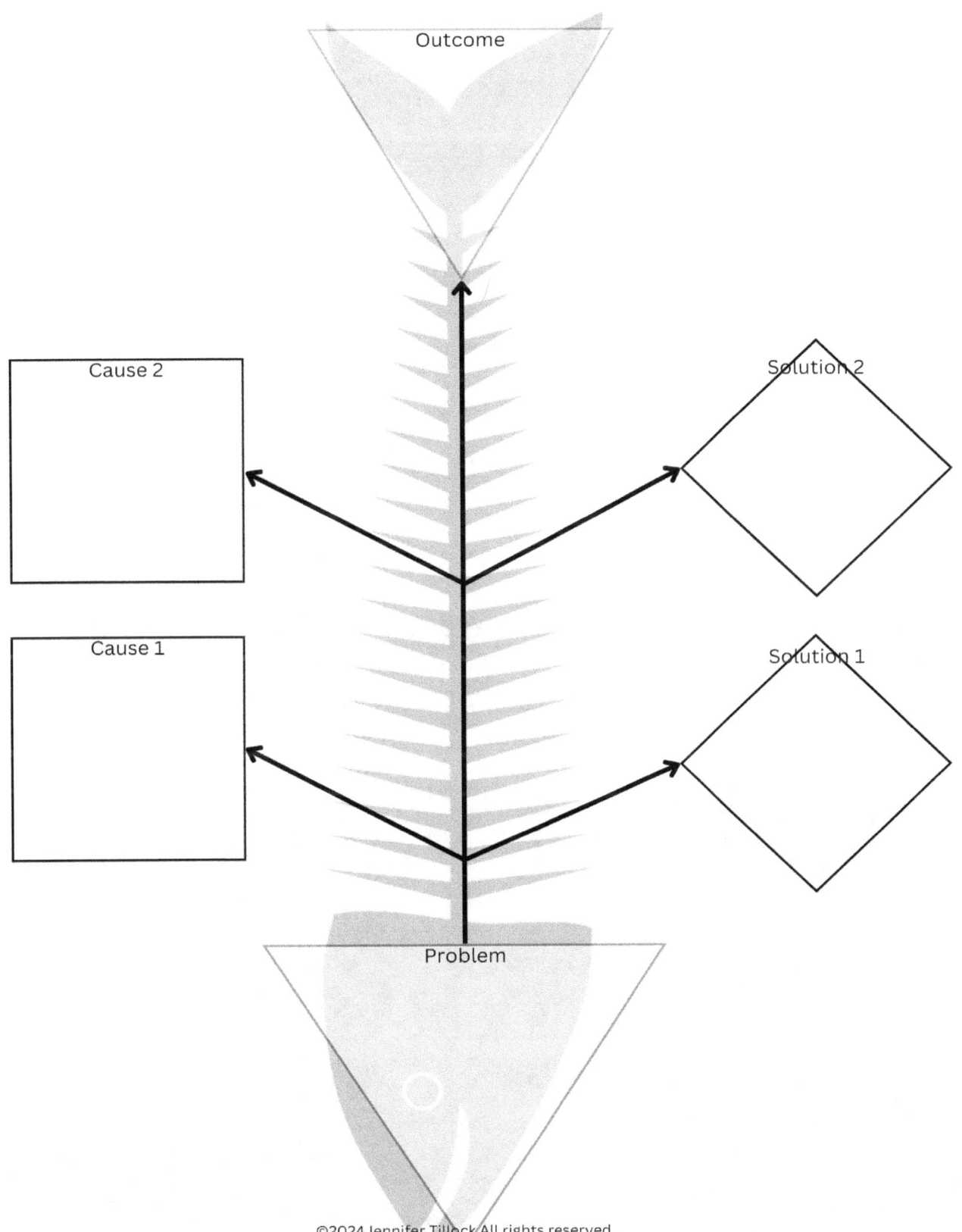

Outcome

Cause 2

Solution 2

Cause 1

Solution 1

Problem

Jennifer Tillock M.S. CCC-SLP

Brainstorm

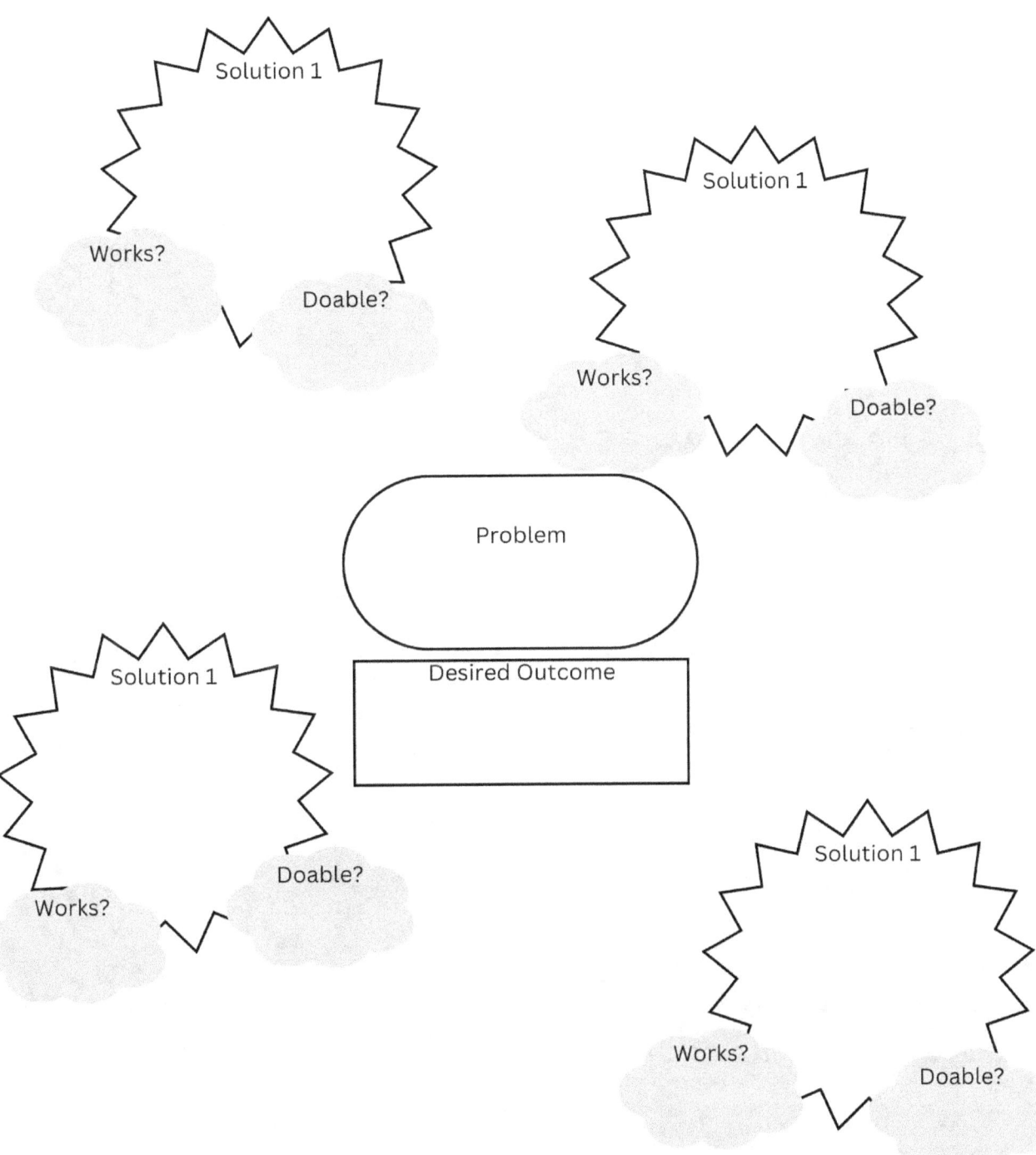

Solution 1

Works?

Doable?

Solution 1

Works?

Doable?

Problem

Desired Outcome

Solution 1

Works?

Doable?

Solution 1

Works?

Doable?

Jennifer Tillock M.S. CCC-SLP

Pros & Cons

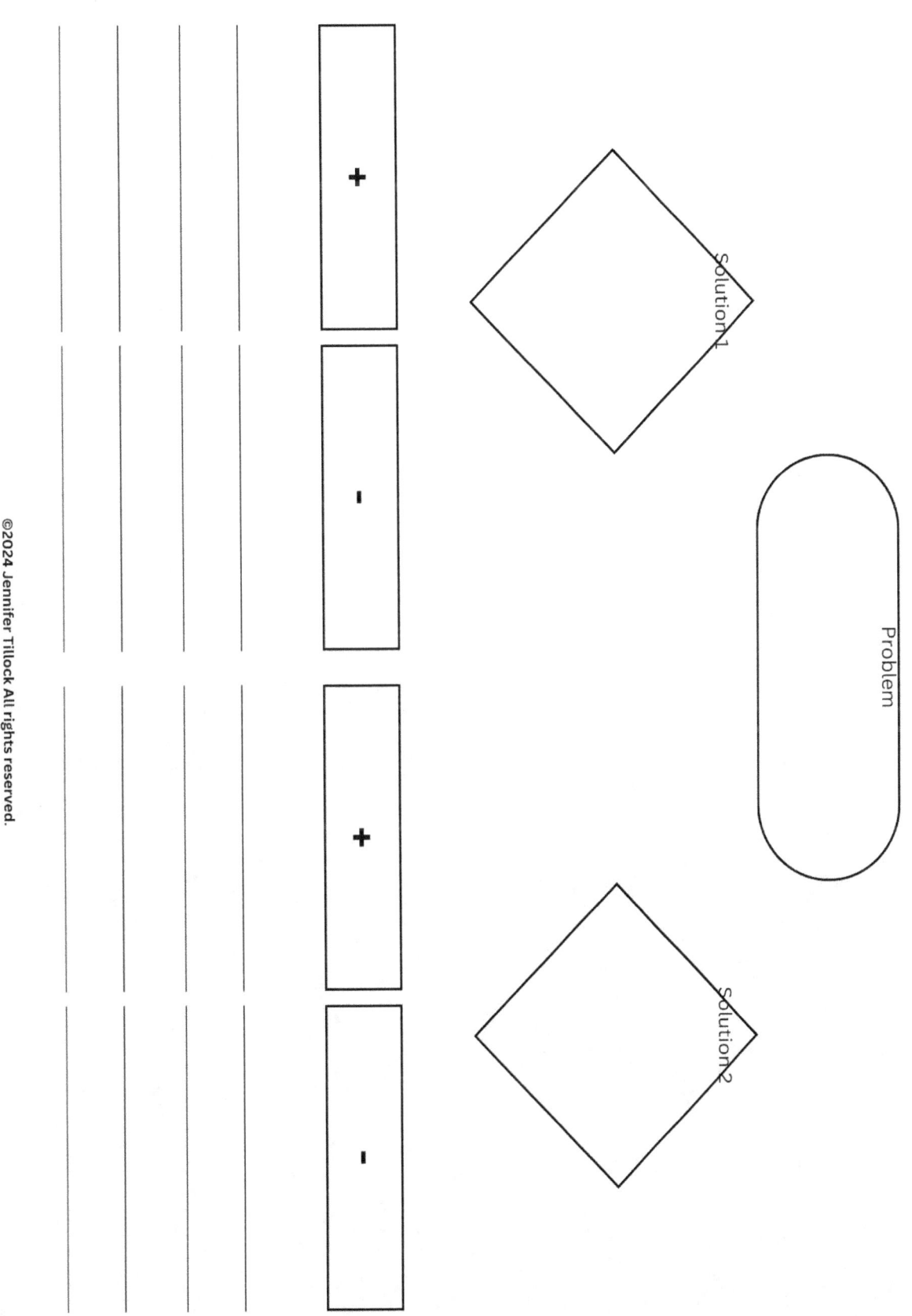

Jennifer Tillock M.S. CCC-SLP

Weighted Pros & Cons

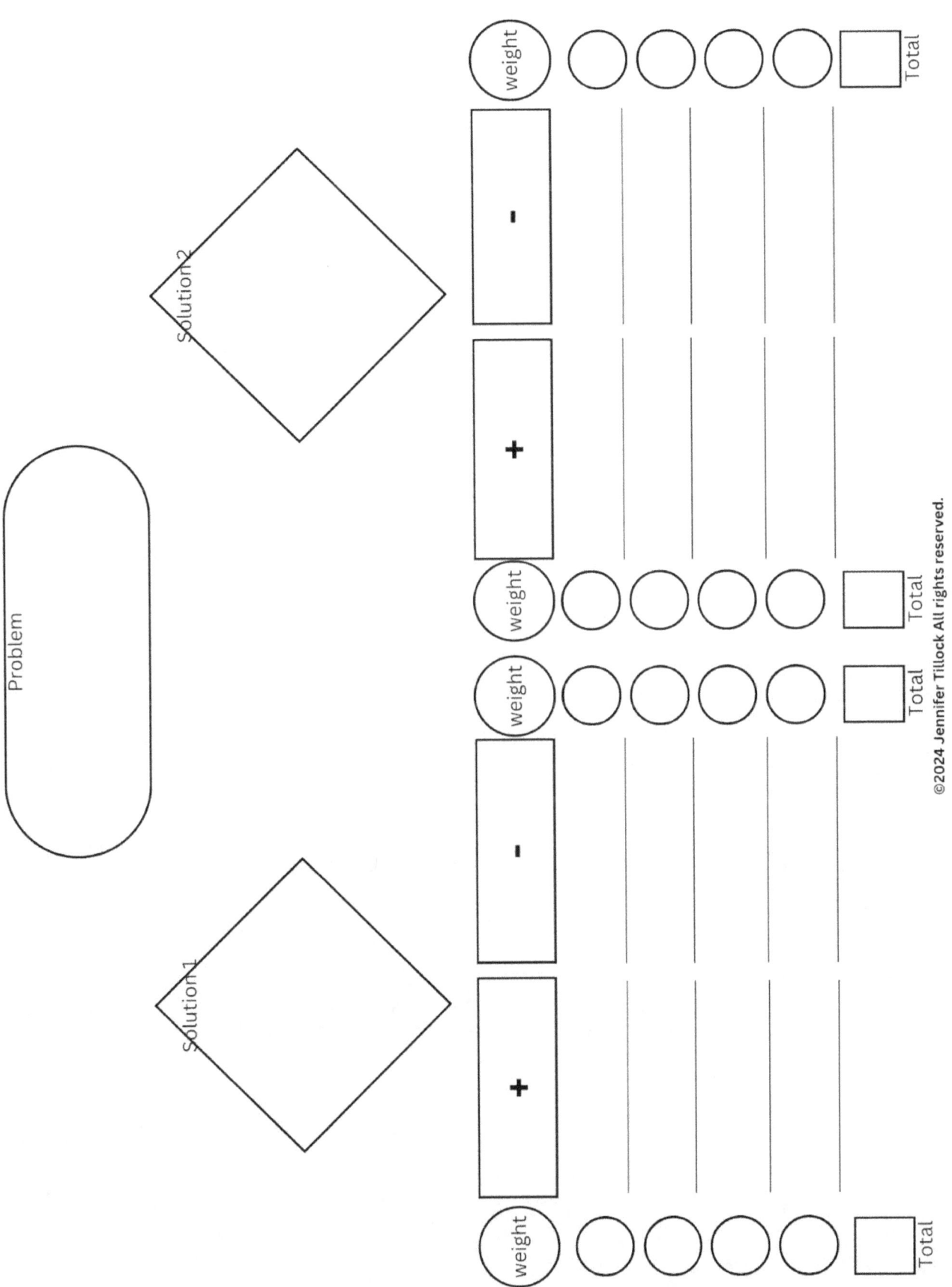

Jennifer Tillock M.S. CCC-SLP

Comic Strip

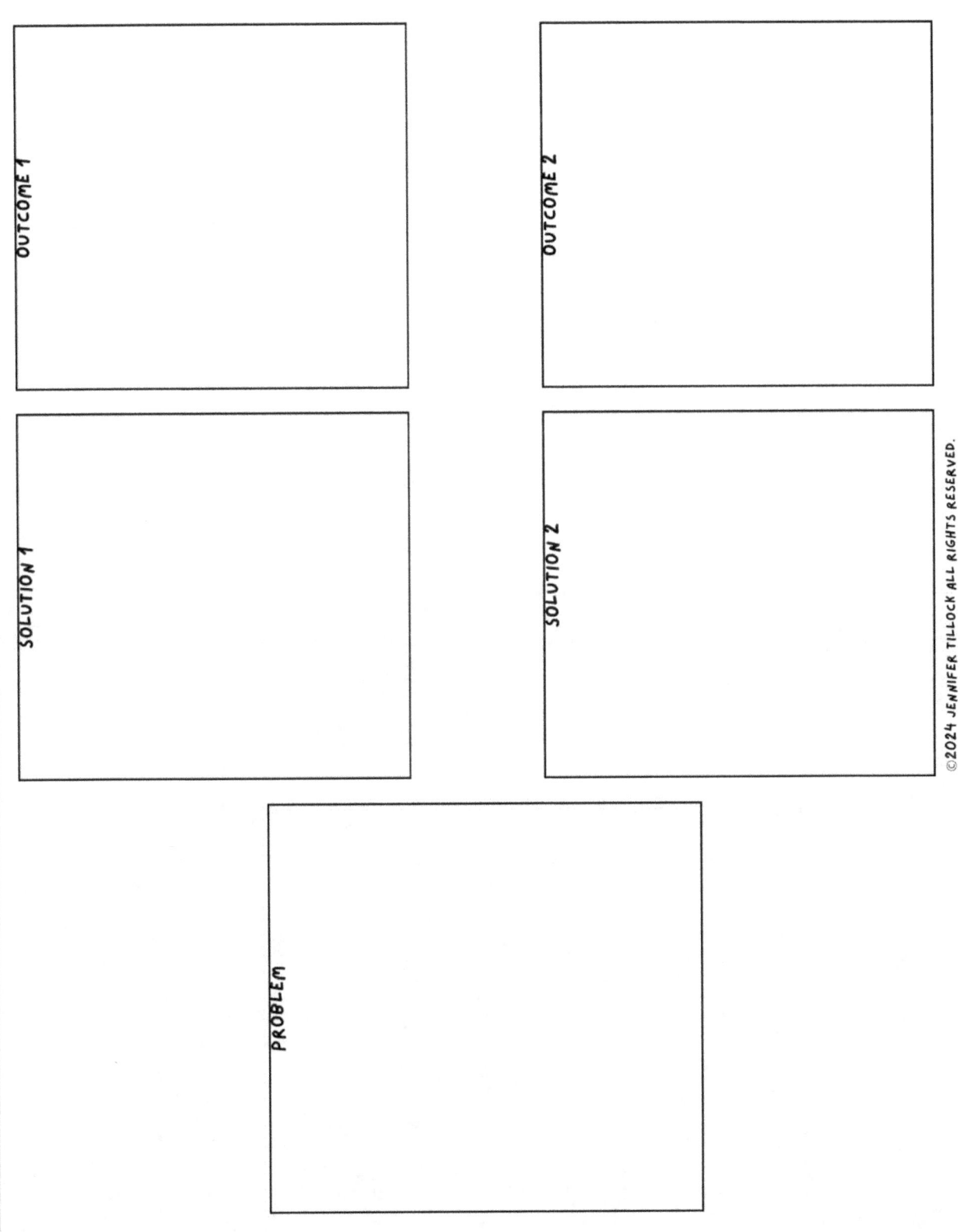

Venn Diagram

Problem

Solution 2

Solution 1

Jennifer Tillock M.S. CCC-SLP

Problem-Solution Tree

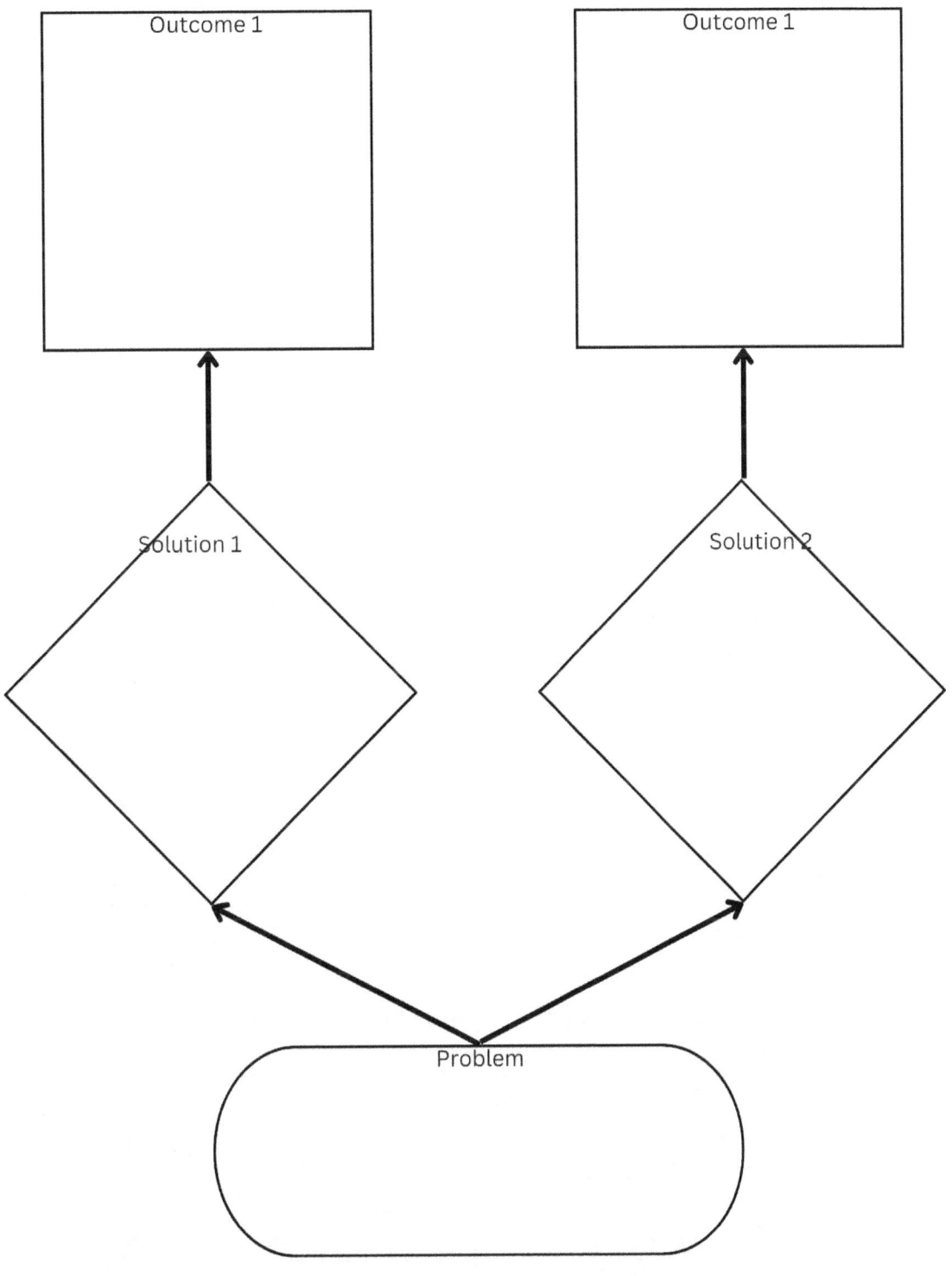

Jennifer Tillock M.S. CCC-SLP

Choose Your Own Adventure

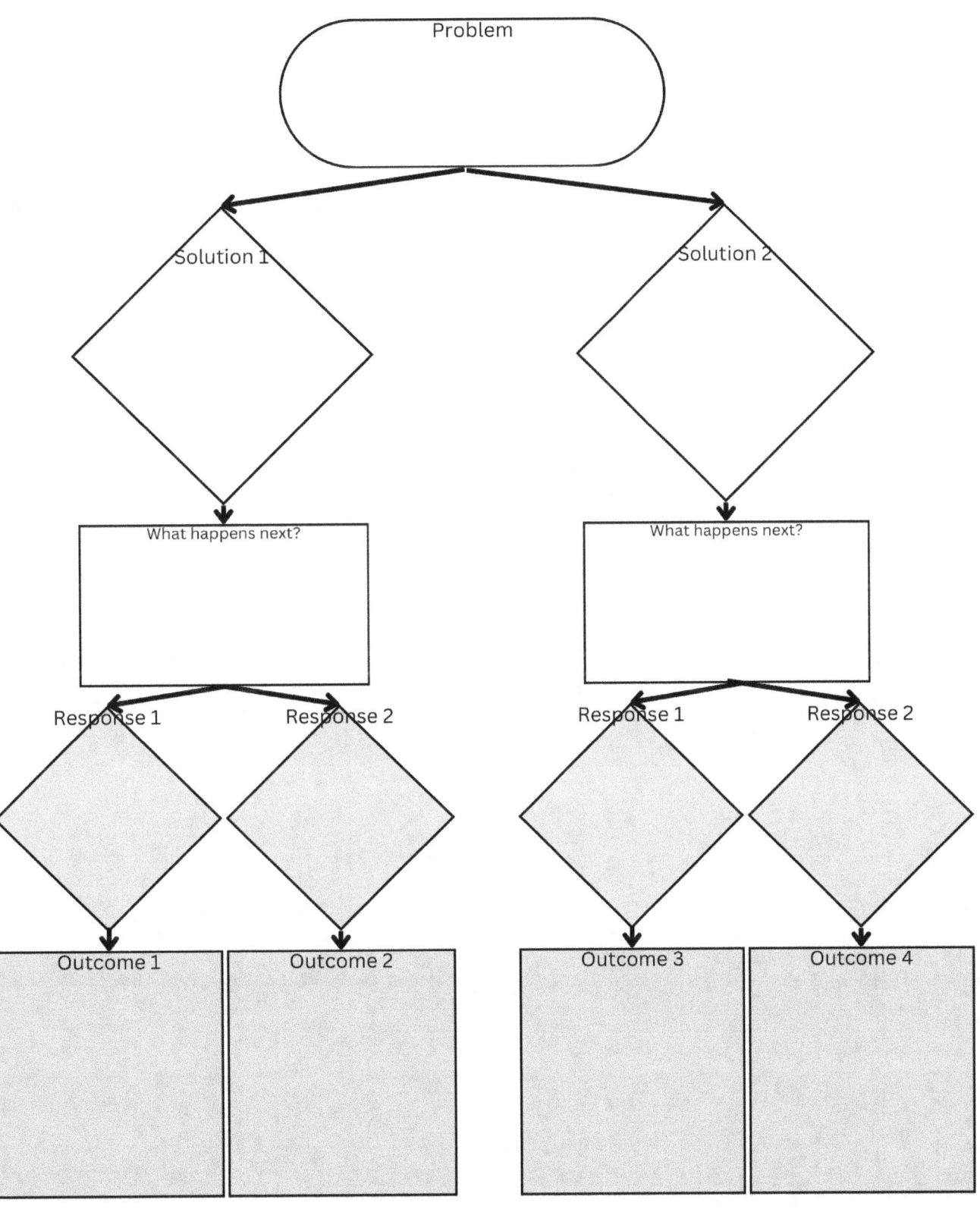

Problem

Solution 1

Solution 2

What happens next?

What happens next?

Response 1

Response 2

Response 1

Response 2

Outcome 1

Outcome 2

Outcome 3

Outcome 4

Jennifer Tillock M.S. CCC-SLP

Problem-Cause-Effect Tree

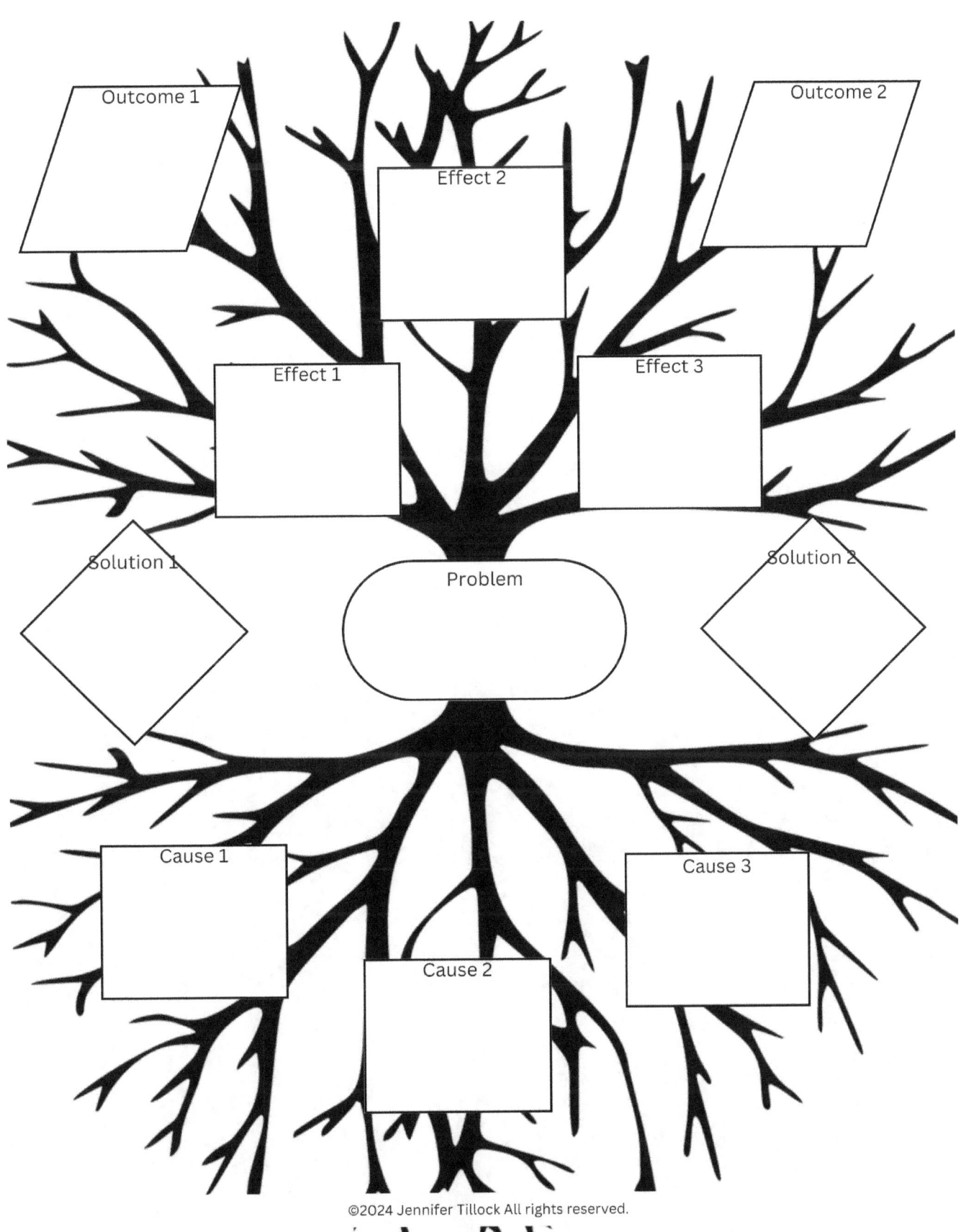

Outcome 1

Outcome 2

Effect 2

Effect 1

Effect 3

Solution 1

Problem

Solution 2

Cause 1

Cause 3

Cause 2

Jennifer Tillock M.S. CCC-SLP

Alphabetical Index

A

B

Jennifer Tillock M.S. CCC-SLP

Jennifer Tillock M.S. CCC-SLP

Q

R

Jennifer Tillock M.S. CCC-SLP

Jennifer Tillock M.S. CCC-SLP